ON THE FIELD WITH . . .

TOM BRADY

ON THE FIELD WITH . . .

TOM BRADY

MATT CHRISTOPHER®

The #1 Sports Series for Kids

Text by Sam Page

LITTLE, BROWN AND COMPANY
New York Boston

Little, Brown and Company

Hachette Book Group
1290 Avenue of the Americas, New York, NY 10104
Visit us at LBYR.com

mattchristopher.com

First Edition: September 2018

Text written by Sam Page

ISBNs: 978-0-316-48606-4 (pbk.), 978-0-316-48607-1 (ebook)

Printed in the United States of America

LSC-H

10 9 8 7 6 5 4 3 2 1

CONTENTS

CHAPTER ONE

★ 1977–1992 ★

SAN MATEO

Before he was the greatest quarterback of all time—before he won more Super Bowl MVP awards than any player in history—Tom Brady was the fourth-best athlete in his own house.

Thomas Edward Patrick Brady Jr. was born on August 3, 1977, to Thomas Brady Sr. and Galynn Patricia Brady. Tom grew up in San Mateo, California, a suburb of San Francisco. He has three older sisters: Maureen, Julie, and Nancy. All three of his sisters would go on to earn collegiate scholarships for sports. Tom's parents encouraged their kids to try all sorts of extracurricular activities, but they all chose athletics. That led to the Brady kids participating in 315 sporting events in one year. Their mom and dad made sure at least one parent attended every one.

Maureen was particularly gifted, setting high school records in softball. She would go on to pitch for Fresno State, where she posted a career 80–31 record and 0.98 ERA. Tom's football career wouldn't truly surpass Maureen's softball achievements until he went pro. That's why for much of his life, Tom Brady was better known as Tommy, the Brady sisters' little brother.

Tom loved and supported his sisters, showing up to their games and cheering. Still, he always wanted to make a name for himself. In ninth grade, he wrote an essay in which he said that he hoped his siblings would one day be known as "Tom Brady's sisters." Surrounded by great athletes, he couldn't help but develop the competitiveness that would become a driving force in his life.

"I started it," Tom Sr. would later tell the *Eagle-Tribune*, a Massachusetts newspaper. "Everything we did—and I mean everything, like running home from church, throwing a rock the farthest—everything was a competition. I guess it made things really fun, at least for the winner."

Things weren't so fun for the loser. Tom Sr. took his son golfing starting when Tommy was a toddler. At one father-son tournament, little Tom cried when his father sank a shot, meaning he wouldn't get to hit it in. On the next hole, Tom Jr. missed a putt on purpose so he would get a few more whacks at the ball.

Another time, before they went to a San Francisco

Giants game, the two Toms played head-to-head. The stakes were high: for every hole Tom Sr. won, Tom Jr. promised to wash his car once. For every hole Tommy won, his dad owed him a dollar. When eleven-year-old Tom Jr. threw his club after a particularly bad shot, his dad told him to wait in the car. Tommy cried but asked his dad to play again after the baseball game. When the second game went a lot like the first, however, the club again went flying.

Away from the links, Tom Jr. kept his temper under control. His mom remembers him as a "carefree" child who kept himself busy with a paper route and altar boy duties at church. (His father had nearly become a priest before settling down and starting a family.) Tom's parents made sure he and his sister understood the values that would make the future Patriots quarterback a fan favorite: treat others well and be humble.

His parents were not teaching Tom these lessons so that he could one day handle his immense fame. They had no reason to believe their Tommy would one day become *the* Tom Brady. He was not a can't-miss athlete or a football prodigy. In fact, Tom did not even play football growing up. A speech from former 49ers offensive lineman Randy Cross convinced Tom's parents that football was dangerous for little kids. So he played other sports until high school, when his quarterbacking career would begin.

Still, there were early signs of Tom Brady the NFL superstar. His family had San Francisco 49ers season tickets during the best era in the franchise's history. The Niners won all five of their championships during Tom's time in San Mateo. Tom's favorite player was Hall of Fame quarterback Joe Montana. When Tom was four years old, his parents took him to Candlestick Park for the NFC Championship game between the 49ers and the Dallas Cowboys.

The 49ers trailed that game by six points with less than a minute to play. Six yards from a touchdown on third down, Montana took the snap under center and rolled out right. Desperate, and with three Cowboys bearing down on him, he heaved a pass to the back of the end zone. There, Dwight Clark leapt and made "The Catch," sending San Francisco to Super Bowl XVI. The crowd erupted. Tom cried because his dad wouldn't buy him a foam finger.

Montana provided more than just inspiration for Tom's football career. He served as a model for how Tom could be great. Like Tom, Montana never possessed the elite athleticism that excites pro scouts. (The 49ers picked him in the third round of the 1979 draft.) But his knowledge of the game and ability to perform under pressure led many to call "Joe Cool" the greatest of all time. He was the only player to ever earn Super Bowl MVP three times—until Tom Brady, who would do it four times.

And even though he did not play organized football until the ninth grade, Tom showed a knack for tossing the pigskin. On a family vacation during his middle school years, he won a bet against his dad by threading a pass through a tire twenty yards away. He then did it again. Tom Sr. was surprised. His son had a gift. Eventually, the rest of the world would realize the same thing.

CHAPTER TWO

★ 1992–1995 ★

HIGH SCHOOL

His coaches and teammates at Junípero Serra High School saw the potential for Tom to one day go pro. He was a superstar known for his strong arm. A coach at a rival school complained once that Tom beat his team single-handedly. Scouts had taken notice of his skills. And Serra had a track record of graduating some of the game's greats. There was no doubt about it: Tom Brady was going to make a great baseball player.

"At the time, I thought his future was in baseball," Pete Jensen, the Serra's baseball coach, told the *Daily News (NY)*. "He could really throw."

He could hit, too. Brady was a catcher known for his power from the left side of the plate. He once hit a home run so far, it hit the team's bus and woke up the driver. And like a true quarterback, he knew how to call a game. Scouts who had shown up to see one of Brady's teammates—center fielder Greg Millichap—soon became interested in the senior first-baseman-turned-catcher who had already committed to play college football.

Those skills led the Montreal Expos (now the Washington Nationals) to pick Brady in the eighteenth round despite his football dream. The Expos were willing to pay him like a third-round pick. They hosted him at a game at Candlestick Park, the very place where Brady had watched Montana's heroics and fallen in love with football. Brady participated in batting practice with the Expos' big leaguers, who were in town to play the Giants. Ultimately, the Montreal players did more to convince Brady to play football, asking him why he'd choose the tough life of a minor league baseball player over the fun of being a football star at a big college.

That college football dream was not always a sure thing. When Tom tried out for the freshman football team at Serra, he wasn't good enough to be the starter. He rode the bench all season for a team that had zero wins, eight losses, and one tie. When his friend who started ahead of him quit football their sophomore year, Tom got his shot to start for the junior varsity squad. He had grown over the summer and began to demonstrate the skills that would make him an NFL legend, including his accuracy and leadership.

"His first game ever, we're down five with two minutes to go and he led us on a game-winning drive," one of Tom's former teammates, John Kirby, would later tell MaxPreps.com. "It was awesome. It's just like he does all the time now. Whenever he was in the huddle, he always seemed in control. He never panicked. He was always motivational, not negative. If we were way down, he'd say, 'C'mon, let's get this going.' He never yelled or blamed."

Serra's football coach, Tom MacKenzie, recognized an arm that could play at the college level. He also understood how much work it would take for the rest of Tom's game to catch up. MacKenzie frankly told Tom and his dad after that sophomore season that the young quarterback would need to work on his poor agility and speed to earn serious looks from Division I college recruiters.

MacKenzie created a workout program for his players called "Bigger, Faster, Stronger." Most high schoolers prefer to work on things they're already good at, rather than try to fix their weaknesses. Tom, ever a hard worker and a perfectionist, took the opposite approach. He relished the opportunity to improve his athleticism. The most notorious of MacKenzie's workouts was the "five-dot drill." Players would have to jump between dots that were painted on the ground in a two-one-two pattern, as if they were playing a very intense, nonstop game of hopscotch. Tom painted the dots in the same pattern on his parents' patio. He shuffled from point to point nonstop for the rest of his high school career. He also invented his own jump-rope workout, which MacKenzie would borrow from Tom and teach to future Serra teams.

Tom's hard work paid off. While the team only went 11–9 during Tom's varsity years, he played well, throwing for over 3,500 yards and thirty touchdowns in those two seasons. MacKenzie tailored the Padres' offense to its star quarterback, using a spread system, which employs lots of receivers to give the passer options.

College scouts took notice—not that they had a choice. Tom's dad had an idea to get his son's name out there: a highlight reel. Tom Sr. created a video that showed Tom's proficiency at throwing a variety of different passes—all set to generic '90s pop music.

"I'd like to introduce my starting quarterback from

this past season, Tom Brady," Tom MacKenzie, clad in a white sweatshirt and standing next to a fidgeting Tom Brady, says in the video. "Tom is a six-foot-four, two-hundred-and-ten-pound athlete that started all ten games for us this past season. He's a big, strong, very durable athlete, who has an excellent work ethic—especially in the off-season—and who does things to try to make himself a better athlete."

Tom Brady Sr. mailed fifty-five copies of that tape to colleges around the country before Tom's junior year. He and Tom also visited football camps at colleges all over the West Coast. The trips provided solid father-son bonding time for the two Toms and gave Tom Jr. yet another opportunity to get the attention of schools.

One person whose attention Tom definitely got was Mike Riley, then offensive coordinator and quarterbacks coach for the University of Southern California. Riley saw past Tom's shortcomings as an athlete—his lack of mobility and arm strength—and recognized his tremendous potential as a leader of both teammates and an offense. During Tom's junior season, Riley visited constantly and developed a relationship with the quarterback and his parents.

Tom seemed to be leaning toward USC. Then Riley got bad news from his head coach: the team had already signed two quarterbacks and no longer had a spot for Tom. Riley flew to San Francisco so he could break the news to Tom in person. One day, he would get another shot at coaching the young quarterback.

Ultimately, Tom's decision came down to the University of California, Berkeley or the University of Michigan. Tom Sr. hoped that his son would choose Cal and stay close to the family. Cal felt they were front-runners for Brady. After a recruiting trip to Ann Arbor, Michigan, though, Tom was enamored with the U of M. Michigan had a tradition of great college quarterbacks, of which Tom was eager to be a part. The Bradys gathered in their living room in San Mateo. Tom broke the bad news to his dad: he was going to commit to Michigan, not Cal.

"I was crying like a baby and said, 'Tommy, this is going to change our relationship,'" Tom Sr. told the *New York Times Magazine* years later. "And he said: 'Dad, I know. It has to.'"

Tom was leaving California, but he wouldn't soon be forgotten. Now, at Serra, Tom's jersey hangs, signed with the inscription "SB 36, SB 38 MVP"—a reference to his first two NFL championship wins. It hangs near that of another former Padre—MLB home run king Barry Bonds. Some figured that Tom would follow Bonds's path to a career in baseball. He was even drafted by the Montreal Expos in the 1995 MLB draft, which recognized Tom as one of the best high school catching prospects in America. But even when Tom decided to say good-bye to the MLB to focus solely on football, no one anticipated Tom would become the Barry Bonds of that sport.

CHAPTER THREE

★ 1996–2000 ★

MICHIGAN

Michigan fans poured into "The Big House," the 100,000-plus-capacity stadium where their beloved Wolverines play football. Coming off a Rose Bowl win and national championship, excitement for football in Ann Arbor was at a peak for the 1998 season. There was a line running half the length of the field to get an autograph from the team's quarterback. They weren't waiting, however, for Tom Brady, the signal caller who would start that season. The fans wanted to meet Tom's backup, incoming freshman Drew Henson, a local high school legend.

This incident embarrassed Tom. But it was typical of his entire experience at the University of Michigan. There was always another quarterback with whom he had to fight for playing time and respect, but Brady never shied away from a challenge or hard work.

Tom's career in maize and blue got off to a bad start. A year before he arrived on campus, the coach who had recruited him, Gary Moeller, had resigned. Michigan's defensive coordinator, Lloyd Carr, took over. Suddenly, Tom found himself competing with six other quarterbacks to impress a boss with whom he had no relationship. He ended up fourth on the depth chart behind second-year freshman Scott Dreisbach, third-year sophomore Brian Griese, and senior Jason Carr. Still, Tom maintained the mentality that he was the best quarterback. He would redshirt during the 1995 season, meaning he would sit the entire season to preserve his eligibility and start a freshman the next season. The next season, in 1996, Tom attempted just five passes as he still sat behind Dreisbach and Griese. The other quarterbacks on the team weren't just going to quit and hand Tom the job, as his competition had in high school.

Finally, before the 1997 season, Tom got his shot. He and fifth-year senior Brian Griese battled for the starter spot. Griese was a former walk-on who had worked his way up on the team. It was the rare time in his career that Tom would be considered the more highly touted, athletically gifted player in a quarterback competition. It was also the rare time he would lose out in such a face-off. Coach Carr decided the more experienced Griese would lead the team.

Tom was ready to give up. He would just never make it at Michigan. Carr, a coach who had no part in recruiting him, clearly had no interest in playing him. So Tom looked into transferring to Cal, where he could get more playing time and be closer to his family. He walked into Carr's office one day and informed his coach of his intention to leave, citing a lack of opportunities. Carr didn't beg him to stay. But he did give Tom some tough love, telling the sophomore backup that leaving would be a big mistake. He told Tom to focus more on his own work and not what other players on the team were doing. Tom thought about what his coach said and came back the next day with a simple message.

"Coach, I've decided that I'm going to stay at Michigan, and I'm going to prove to you that I'm a great quarterback."

Like he had done with the five-dot drill back home, Tom spent time away from the practice field working to get better. He woke up at the crack of dawn to run up and down the stadium stairs alone before going to train with his teammates. The hard work paid off—by January he passed Dreisbach as the team's number-two quarterback.

Meanwhile, Griese made the most of the starter's

role. Michigan entered the season ranked number fourteen in the nation by the Associated Press poll. By the end of the season, they ranked number one after going undefeated and beating Washington State in the Rose Bowl. They were considered co-national champions with Nebraska, who finished atop the coach's poll.

"The pressure of defending a national championship is pretty tough, but it's a position we all want to be in," Tom told a reporter before the 1998 season began.

Tom faced more pressure than just the high expectations of fans. As the autograph incident at the start of the season showed, the departure of Griese did not spell the end of the quarterback competition. Drew Henson had starred for a high school just outside of Ann Arbor. He boasted the speed and strength Tom lacked. Henson had even been taken higher in Major League Baseball's draft than Tom: ninety-seventh overall, by the Yankees. He would even play with the Yankees' minor league teams when school was out at Michigan.

"When Drew Henson gets here, there isn't any question he will add a dimension we don't have,"

Carr told the *Detroit Free Press*. "It's open competition. I expect him to compete."

Tom wasn't interested in what Henson had done in high school. He had worked hard to justify his decision not to transfer to Cal. No true freshman, no matter how athletic and good at baseball, was going to take his spot.

"The hype ends today when the doors close and everyone leaves," Tom said to the *Detroit News*. "To be the best, you have to beat out the best. I've fought long and hard to be in this position, and I don't plan to give it up."

Indeed, Tom did win the starting job. But his title defense started poorly. The Wolverines lost their first two games to Notre Dame and Syracuse, two opponents ranked lower than them. During the Syracuse loss, down 24–7, Tom tried to rally his team by yelling, "We are going to win this game!" His teammates didn't respond. How could they treat him as their undisputed leader when he wasn't even their undisputed quarterback? Sure enough, he was benched for Henson in the fourth quarter.

To fend off Henson, Tom only worked harder. He studied game film all night. He went over every broken play with his teammates. Soon, he became a master of recognizing defenses. His intensity even carried over to the mini-golf course, where Tom dominated his teammates.

After those opening losses, Michigan went on an eight-game winning streak and finished the season 10–3. Tom led his team to a win over higher-ranked Arkansas in the Citrus Bowl. He finished his first season as a starter with 2,427 yards, fourteen touchdowns, and ten interceptions. He set a school record with 214 completions.

Still, just days after winning the Citrus Bowl, however, Tom was in the newspaper defending his starting job for 1999. His coach had been quoted discussing the idea of Henson starting in his second year. Ultimately, Carr decided on an unusual arrangement: Tom would play the first quarter of games and Henson would play the second quarter. How well they each played determined who got to play the second half. Tom was a senior and a leader on the team. But the Michigan fans wanted to see their star recruit, and Henson could always decide to leave for the Yankees.

In four of the first five games of the 1999 season, Tom outplayed Henson and took the field for the second half. In the sixth game of the season, against rival Michigan State, Henson went in for the third quarter but played poorly. Tom subbed back in and threw for 241 yards in the last eighteen minutes of the game. The Wolverines weren't able to come back, but they had come close. That was the end of the double quarterback system. Tom had proven that being a quarterback was about more than being strong. Preparation, intelligence, and calmness under pressure had won out.

Three weeks later, number-sixteen Michigan played number-six Penn State. The Wolverines found themselves down 27–17. Tom kept getting hit by opposing defensive linemen. When he returned to the huddle, wide receiver David Terrell pointed out that Tom had blood on his face. "D. T., just do your job," Tom shot back. Little did he know "do your job" would one day be the mantra of his NFL coach. Tom did his job, and Michigan won, 31–27. People started calling him the "Comeback Kid"—one of his idol Joe Montana's nicknames.

Michigan finished their regular season 9–2 and ranked eighth in the country. They drew number-five Alabama in the Orange Bowl in Miami. Alabama got out to an early 14–0 lead. Then the Comeback Kid went to work. On Alabama's twenty-eight-yard line with 1:04 left in the half, Tom sat back in the shotgun and threw a deep strike to Terrell. Touchdown.

Early in the third quarter, Tom stared down a blitz on third and eight and found Terrell twenty yards across midfield. Terrell lost his defender and ran the remaining length of the field for the score. 14–14.

The Tide would answer with two touchdowns of their own to jump ahead 28–14. Tom didn't panic. Midway through the third quarter, he put together a nine-play, seventy-two-yard drive, capped off by yet another touchdown pass to Terrell. The Wolverine defense stepped up on Alabama's next drive to get the ball back to Tom. Suddenly, Michigan's offense was driving with all the momentum against a tired defense. Despite two dropped potential touchdowns from his receivers, Tom led his team down to the red zone, where they punched it in with a run play. The Comeback Kid had lived up to his name: 28–28.

Tom put his team to win late in the fourth quarter. With two seconds left, Michigan had a chance at a thirty-six-yard field goal to break the tie. Tom was the holder. The snap came. The clock went to 0:00. Alabama blocked the kick! Tom scrambled for the loose ball and threw up a desperate pass. No one caught it. The game was headed to overtime.

In overtime, each team got the ball at their opponent's twenty-five with a chance to score. Michigan went first, so if they scored a touchdown, Alabama had to answer with a touchdown. If they made a field goal or failed to get any points, Alabama could win with a score. Brady needed just one play. He faked a hand-off before rolling out and finding tight end Shawn Thompson wide open. Touchdown!

Alabama answered with a play-action pass of their own, finding a receiver uncovered in the end zone. They just needed to kick an extra point to force a second overtime. But they missed! Michigan won the first overtime game in the history of the Orange Bowl. Tom had thrown for 369 yards and four touchdowns in the biggest game of his life so far. He had proven himself as Michigan's best quarterback and as a clutch performer. Despite not always being treated as such, he was now part of a legacy of great passers to wear the maize and blue.

"The challenges I think toughened me up a lot," Tom would later tell Boston.com about his Michigan career. "Growing up in California and going to Ann Arbor and competing with those guys for as long as we did, it was a great experience. I took a lot of those things that I learned and brought them to the professional level. I was lucky to learn a lot of lessons at nineteen and twenty and twenty-one that a lot of guys don't learn until they're twenty-three or twenty-four or later when it's too late."

CHAPTER FOUR

★ 2000 ★

THE DRAFT

Tom Brady can still name from memory all six quarterbacks taken ahead of him in the 2000 NFL draft. He even remembers where they each went to school and the rounds in which they were taken.

Chad Pennington, Giovanni Carmazzi, Chris Redman, Tee Martin, Marc Bulger, and Spergon Wynn. How many of those names do you recognize?

In the eyes of NFL general managers, though, Tom had surprisingly little going for him leading up to the draft. Despite the great end to his career in Michigan, pro scouts did not regard Tom as a top prospect. And Tom did himself no favors when he showed up to the NFL scouting combine, the yearly event in which draft-eligible prospects complete a variety of workouts and tests to give interested teams a sense of their athleticism.

A photo of a shirtless Tom checking in at the event became infamous for how unathletic he looked. The exercises themselves did nothing to fix that first impression. Wearing a baggy T-shirt and plain sneakers, Tom ran the forty-yard dash, a popular measure of speed, in 5.28 seconds. By comparison, Chad Clifton, an offensive tackle who would be taken in the second round of that same draft by the Packers, ran the forty in 5.05 seconds. Clifton was listed at 330 pounds.

Brady also attended a predraft workout hosted by his childhood team, the San Francisco 49ers. Steve Young, the Hall of Fame quarterback who had succeeded Joe Montana, had just retired. The 49ers needed a new franchise QB to take the torch of Montana and Young, who made San Francisco an unrivaled passing offense for two decades. San Francisco had won five Super Bowls with those two players.

Legendary former Niners coach Bill Walsh had engineered the Niners' West Coast offense, which was perfect for accurate, cerebral passers like Tom. He attended the workout, too. Tom didn't impress. The 49ers picked two quarterbacks in that draft that weren't Tom Brady.

Making things worse for Tom was the perception of his time at Michigan. Despite all of Tom's success, head coach Lloyd Carr had seemed eager to replace Tom with Drew Henson. For a quarterback without speed or impressive arm strength, not even having the full support of his college coach was killer.

There was, however, at least one team that seemed interested in the Michigan graduate. Mike Riley, the man who had tried to recruit Tom to USC, was now the head coach of the San Diego Chargers. The Chargers' quarterback was Jim Harbaugh, a Michigan alum nearing the end of his career. Riley was still a fan of Brady for all the reasons he had been back in 1995. He recognized the quarterback's intangibles: his leadership ability, intelligence, and calmness under pressure.

Tom watched the draft at his parents' house in San Mateo. The first two rounds went by and he wasn't picked. In round three, the 49ers took Giovanni Carmazzi, a quarterback known for his athleticism.

"We were just hurt," Tom Brady Sr. recalled to ESPN. "We kind of took it personally, if you will."

Still, even if Tom was not going to play for his hometown team, maybe he could still stay in California playing for the Chargers. Every time San Diego came up, the Bradys waited for their phone to ring. It never did. Riley had been overruled, again—this time by his general manager.

Tom was upset. He grabbed a baseball bat and

walked outside. He was ready to drive away when his mom, Galynn, walked outside to get him. Bill Belichick from the New England Patriots was calling.

The Patriots were concerned about the fact that Michigan seemed to have favored Henson over Tom. But in the sixth round, the value seemed too good to pass up. Patriots quarterback coach Dick Rehbein had scouted Tom at Michigan and saw a winner who had led his team to multiple impressive comeback wins. According to ESPN, Rehbein had told his wife, "Twenty years from now people will know the name Tom Brady." Despite not needing a quarterback—their starter, Drew Bledsoe, was just twenty-seven—New England took a flier on Tom.

And though he was the 199th player taken in the draft, Tom's confidence didn't waver. When he first met Patriots owner, Robert Kraft, he had a simple message: "I'm the best decision this organization has ever made."

Tom doesn't remember the name of every quarterback taken ahead because of a grudge he holds against them. He sees them as a reminder that the thirty-one teams that passed on him made a big mistake.

CHAPTER FIVE

★ 2000–2001 ★

WELCOME TO NEW ENGLAND

When he arrived in New England, Tom found himself in a familiar spot: on the bottom of the depth chart. Since he had gone to the Patriots and not a more QB-needy team, Tom would have to relive his freshman season in Michigan and fight for more practice reps. Veteran John Friesz was Drew Bledsoe's backup, and the Pats had drafted another young quarterback the year before named Michael Bishop. Tom, however, had learned an important lesson the day he threatened to transfer out of Michigan. His college coach, Lloyd Carr, had told him to just worry about himself. So that's what he was going to do on his new team.

"I am going out there every day, trying to get better and see how good I can possibly be because there are a lot of great quarterbacks here," Tom told the *Boston Globe*. "It is so competitive that you just have to go out and worry about yourself, worry about completing balls when you are in, and hopefully get better each day."

Tom impressed the coaches with his preparedness, work ethic, and confidence. With three quarterbacks already on the roster, many expected the Patriots to cut Tom and send him to their practice squad. But if they did that, any other team would have an opportunity to claim him off waivers. To ensure he did not lose Tom, Patriots coach Bill Belichick did something unusual: he carried four quarterbacks on the roster despite only dressing three for game days. Tom may have been the fourth quarterback on the depth chart, but the Patriots saw enough potential in him to "waste" a roster spot for an entire season just to ensure he stuck around.

That didn't mean his coaches believed they had a future Hall of Famer on their hands necessarily. One day, when Tom found himself alone in a team meeting room, he peeked inside a coach's notebook. There he found an evaluation of himself: "Slow on reads. Slow to react. Doesn't deliver the ball on time." He would never have elite speed. He could, however, become faster at reading opposing defenses. And that meant time spent tirelessly watching film.

The film on the 2000 New England Patriots couldn't be fun to watch. In Bill Belichick's first season as head coach, the team finished 5–11. Its offense ranked near the bottom of the league. Despite the team's game-day performance, Tom was slowly moving up the depth chart in practice. Tom spent time in the weight room trying to get stronger. He also became the team's most devoted film student, and he became an expert at recognizing when defenses were preparing to blitz.

All that hard work paid off on Thanksgiving Day 2000, when the Patriots got creamed by the Lions in Detroit. Belichick decided to pull Bledsoe late in the blowout. And it wasn't Friesz or Bishop that went in, but Tom. In his first NFL action, Tom attempted three passes and completed one—for six yards. It was a modest beginning to a legendary career. But going from sixth-round draft pick to mop-up duty in week thirteen was a meteoric rise.

By the time the season ended, Tom had earned the trust and admiration of his coaches. However, people outside the organization who only knew his predraft scouting report and not his work ethic off the field, doubted him. A *Boston Herald* story evaluating each player's chance of making next year's roster said Tom "needs to show he's got a legitimate NFL arm," while Michael Bishop more kindly said, "He gives the team a different look and has potential."

During the off-season, Drew Bledsoe re-signed with the team for ten years and $103 million. It was the biggest contract in NFL history. It might have seemed like the deal closed off any future for Tom in New England. Tom, however, kept focusing on himself and working hard. As Bishop went off to play in NFL Europe in the spring, Tom stayed in Foxborough, Massachusetts, and became a leader for the team's off-season workout program. He added fifteen pounds of muscle and became an expert on New England's offense.

He and Belichick had similar goals. Both newcomers to the organization last season, they were disappointed with the team's work ethic. Belichick addressed the problem by reshaping his roster to add more "high-character" players. Tom did his part, leading by example with the way he prepared.

Tom's improvement was obvious. On one play in training camp, he looked right at veteran safety Lawyer Milloy and fooled him with a pump fake before throwing to another target. After the play, Milloy had a simple message for the second-year QB, "Good job; don't do it again."

Then, during the preseason, tragedy struck the Patriots. Quarterbacks coach Dick Rehbein, the man who had scouted Tom at Michigan and convinced the Patriots to draft him, died suddenly at age forty-five from heart failure. His death affected all the quarterbacks on the roster.

"My dad would talk about Tom Brady almost as if Tom was his own kid," Rehbein's daughter Betsy would later tell ESPN.com. "He would talk about Tom driving this yellow Jeep Wrangler, making fun of this little boy he was watching grow up."

Rehbein's death meant that Belichick would have to take a more hands-on role in coaching his passers. The team had signed veteran Damon Huard to be Bledsoe's backup in the coming season. They also waived Bishop, seemingly creating a clear hierarchy of quarterbacks. At the beginning of training camp, Belichick called Huard the number-two quarterback. As the summer continued, however, he spoke less definitively. Tom had forced a competition for the job.

Then, during the team's preseason games, Tom did something no one expected. He didn't just outplay Huard—he outplayed *Bledsoe*. He completed thirty-one of fifty-four passes for two touchdowns and zero interceptions. The Patriots weren't ready to bench their $100-million QB for an unproven player. But Belichick did announce that Tom had beaten Huard for the backup job. The notoriously tight-lipped Belichick even allowed himself to gush about his young passing prospect.

"I don't think there was any question in anybody's mind that Tom had clearly taken over the leadership of [last year's rookies]—offense, defense, everybody that was involved," the coach said. "I think he was well respected."

Tom did not compare himself to the other quarterbacks on the roster. He simply talked constantly about preparation. He wanted to make sure when he got his big NFL opportunity that he took full advantage. Few could have predicted how soon that opportunity came.

The Patriots lost their first game of the season to the Bengals in a blowout. Then in Game 2 against the Jets, one play changed the entire trajectory of the Patriots' franchise. With his team down 10–3 in the fourth quarter, Bledsoe tried to run for the sticks on third down. As he dashed up the sideline, New York linebacker Mo Lewis knocked him out of bounds with a bone-crunching hit to his upper body.

"It was the hardest hit I've ever heard," Tom would later say.

Bledsoe was dazed on the sideline. Tom was in. The situation seemed like a game at Michigan with

Drew Henson—Tom would arrive in the fourth quarter to save the day. The Patriots drove forty-one yards down the field. Tom even ran for nine yards on one play! His Hail Mary pass to tie it late, however, fell just short.

Tom had not blown his one shot. Bledsoe's injuries proved more serious than anyone realized at the time. He checked into the hospital with internal bleeding. With rumors swirling about the exact extent of his injuries, no one knew how long the quarterback would be out. Tom Brady would lead the Pats' offense for the foreseeable future.

"I really don't think I'm going to be standing here week after week talking about the problems that Tom Brady had," Belichick said. "I have confidence in him."

His teammates also believed in Tom. While they didn't expect him to be Drew Bledsoe, a three-time Pro Bowler and former first-overall pick, they respected how Tom went about his business.

"There's nothing you can do to really shake him," said wide receiver Troy Brown. "He's a California guy. He's cool."

Tom's first NFL start came against Peyton Manning's Colts. Peyton and Tom would become rivals competing for the mantle of the NFL's best quarterback. In this game, however, Manning was a superstar and Tom a player just trying to get his footing. The coaches tried to make things easy for Tom. The team ran the ball thirty-nine times and Tom attempted just twenty-three passes. Tom managed the game well, not throwing any interceptions. The Patriots' defense, meanwhile, picked Manning off three times as the Pats won 44–13. Tom was 1–0.

His second game didn't go as well. The Pats lost 30–10 to the Dolphins in Miami. Tom threw for just eighty-six yards and fumbled a ball that was run in for a touchdown by the defense. After the game, however, Tom showed his leadership ability. Walking off the field with Lawyer Milloy, a defensive captain, Tom discussed how the entire team needed to work harder before games. He then delivered the kind of fiery postgame speech more typical of a veteran quarterback late in the season.

"You can't go out and practice average on Wednesday and average on Thursday and okay on Friday and expect to come out on Sunday and play good," Tom said. He later added, "I'm pretty even tempered, but I hate to lose. I hate to lose."

The little boy who had once thrown his golf club

had just shown the public what would make him so successful: his competitiveness. In practice that week, Belichick buried a ball, an act symbolic of the team's need to move on from the Miami game. Tom stomped on the ground where the ball was buried.

Tom's emphasis on preparation would prove important in week five against the Chargers. With less than nine minutes left in the game, San Diego scored on a fumble to go up 26–16. It looked like New England would be 1–4 and well on their way to another losing season.

The Comeback Kid had other ideas. He led the team to consecutive scoring drives—first a field goal, and then a touchdown pass with forty seconds left on the clock. Then in overtime, Tom recognized a formation in the San Diego defense the Patriots had practiced for. They were going to blitz. He audibled and threw a deep pass to receiver David Patten. The Chargers were called for pass interference, and the Patriots had the field position to kick a game-winning field goal.

"I can't say enough about Tom Brady," Belichick said afterward. "He runs the team well."

So he kept running the team. Starting in week ten, doctors cleared Drew Bledsoe to play. But Tom was 5–2 since starting over. Belichick made the controversial decision to bench Bledsoe for the rest of the season. Bledsoe was the team's franchise quarterback who was being paid millions of dollars. But Tom Brady was a sensation. He had definitely made the most of his opportunity. The player who had fought for playing time at every level suddenly found himself the undisputed starting quarterback of an NFL team.

Tom made Belichick look good. After narrowly losing to the Super Bowl–favorite St. Louis Rams (who have since moved to Los Angeles), the Patriots closed out their season on a six-game winning streak. A season after finishing 5–11 under Bledsoe, the Pats went 11–5 under Tom Brady. The quarterback who never cracked under pressure was headed to football's biggest stage: the NFL playoffs.

CHAPTER SIX

★ 2002 ★

UNDERDOG CHAMPS

These days, the New England Patriots are a dynasty. Once upon a time, however, they were scrappy underdogs in need of a break.

On January 19, 2002, in their divisional round playoff game against the Oakland Raiders, the Pats trailed by 10–13 with less than two minutes to go. In its last game before demolition, Foxboro Stadium was covered in snow. The Pats were driving, with the ball on the forty-two-yard line. Would Mother Nature stop the Comeback Kid?

Tom took the snap on first and ten. The Raiders' defense attacked with a zone blitz. Tom focused on the left side of the field, which had looked vacant presnap. He changed his mind and pulled the ball back down. Meanwhile, streaking down his blind side was Oakland cornerback Charles Woodson, a former teammate of Tom's at Michigan. Woodson hit Tom from behind and the ball came loose. The Raiders recovered. Tom walked to the sideline disgusted. The Patriots' season was over, because he fumbled.

Or so he thought. The referees reviewed the play. They decided that because Tom's arm was coming forward with the ball when he fumbled, it was technically a forward pass. The "tuck rule" is one of the most infamous calls in NFL history. But the Pats would take it. Tom made one more thirteen-yard pass, then the Pats had to try the game-tying field goal. New England kicker Adam Vinatieri lined up from forty-five yards away. He booted the ball, barely visible flying through the snow. Good!

In sudden-death overtime, the Patriots got the ball first. Tom completed all eight passes he threw before handing the ball off four times. Vinatieri lined up again from twenty-three yards out. The football sailed through the uprights! Tom was going to play in the AFC Championship game.

Playing in Pittsburgh against the Steelers, the Patriots were serious underdogs. But no one who saw Tom Brady walk through the tunnel toward the field would have gotten that impression. "We're coming, baby!" the quarterback yelled, clapping his hands.

Unfortunately, the Steelers were coming, too, and coming for Tom. Late in the second quarter, with the Pats up 7–3, a Steelers pass rusher hit Tom in the legs as he threw. Tom's legs bent awkwardly over his tackler and he yelled in pain. Brady remained down in the backfield. Drew Bledsoe came in and, on that very same drive, threw his first touchdown pass of the season.

Belichick stuck with Bledsoe, and the veteran delivered. New England hung on to win 24–17. They were AFC Champions. For Tom, however, sitting on the sideline and watching his team win a big game was not wholly satisfying. He would be ready for the Super Bowl.

In the week leading up to the Super Bowl, the Patriots' quarterback controversy returned. Had Bledsoe gotten his job back? Would Tom be physically able to play? On Wednesday, Tom finally practiced. He would start in Super Bowl XXXVI in New Orleans, against the St. Louis Rams. Known for his cool, Tom wasn't going to let the fanfare surrounding the "Big Game" distract him. Before kickoff, Tom took a nap.

When the game started, the Patriots' offense looked a little sleepy. The Pats punted on their first four drives. The Rams hit an early field goal and New England's defense answered with a pick-six (an interception returned for a touchdown).

Finally, running the two-minute drill right before halftime, New England drove into the red zone. Here, Tom's intense preparation and study of opponents' habits would pay off. He knew Rams cornerback Dexter McCleon would play his man right on the goal line. Tom pump-faked a pass right on the goal line. McCleon bit, allowing David Patten to get behind him. Tom lofted the ball, which Patten caught midair while diving. Touchdown! The Patriots led 14–3 at halftime in the Super Bowl.

New England kicked a field goal after halftime to go up two touchdowns, but St. Louis soon proved why they were preseason title favorites. Kurt Warner rushed and threw for touchdowns in the fourth quarter to tie the game. The Patriots would get the ball back with 1:21 left in the game and the score tied, 17–17.

"Now with no time-outs, I think that the Patriots—with this field position—you have to just run the clock out, you have to just play for overtime," said John Madden on the Fox broadcast of the game.

It's true the Patriots had no time-outs and were stuck on their own seventeen-yard line. They also had, however, a young QB who lived for the big moments. Tom asked offensive coordinator Charlie

Weis if the coaches wanted to run the clock out or try some plays to set up a game-winning field goal. Weis gave him the green light to try to win the game.

Tom evaded a ferocious pass rush to check the ball down to running back J. R. Redmond on the first play. As Madden continued to protest, Tom got right back into the shotgun without huddling and took another snap. He threw another short pass to Redmond, who spiked the ball to stop the clock with forty-one seconds left.

Tom threw to Redmond again on second down, and he got the first down and ran out of bounds to stop the clock. The Rams blitzed on first down. Tom smartly threw the ball away to avoid being sacked. Twenty-nine seconds left. On the next play, Tom hit Troy Brown for twenty-three yards, their biggest gain of the drive. Tom made one more pass to Jermaine Wiggins for six yards and then had to spike the ball to stop the clock.

"I'll tell you, what Tom Brady just did gives me goose bumps," Madden said.

Six seconds remained on the clock. Tom had driven his team down the field with no margin of error and given Vinatieri a shot at a forty-eight-yard field goal to win the game. The snap and hold were clean. Vinatieri got it up. No doubt. It went right down the middle. Players spilled onto the field from the Patriots' sideline, hugging, jumping, and, in one case, even pretending to make a snow angel in the end zone. The New England Patriots won their first Super Bowl in franchise history. Twenty-four-year-old Tom Brady led the game-winning drive with no time-outs.

Tom, clad in a Super Bowl champion T-shirt and with his hat on backward, pointed at his sisters sitting in the stands. He put his hands on his head and laughed in disbelief. The Brady sisters' brother, Tommy, was a Super Bowl champion. And now they could be known as Tom Brady's sisters.

CHAPTER SEVEN

★ 2002–2003 ★

GETTING BACK

After New England's improbable run to Super Bowl XXXVI, everyone wanted to know: who is the next Tom Brady?

Perhaps Chad Pennington, the Jets quarterback selected in the same draft as Tom. Another article speculated that Giants backup Jesse Palmer could "pull a Brady" and come out of nowhere to win a Super Bowl. After Tom got off to a slow start in the preseason, the newspapers even wondered if someone on the Patriots would pull a Tom Brady on Tom Brady.

Tom set out to prove that he was one of a kind. Stories circulated that Tom had been working out in an otherwise deserted stadium just weeks after the season ended. (The Patriots would move into their new home, Gillette Stadium, this off-season.) Tom wanted his Super Bowl victory to be the start of something great, not the biggest achievement of a sixth-round draft pick that exceeded expectations.

It was a trying off-season, however. In June 2002, Patriots offensive coordinator Charlie Weis underwent surgery. When Tom came to check on him after the operation, he found his coach in critical condition—there had been complications from the procedure. Tom stayed in the hospital until Weis's family got there. Weis went into a coma and nearly died. When he pulled through, it was Tom who helped him keep going.

"Tommy was one of the reasons why I got back to work quicker than you normally would . . . because of his pushing," Weis told NFL Network in a documentary about the Pats' 2003 season. "Mentally and emotionally, he was an uplifting person for me."

The Patriots were looking to the young quarterback to uplift their entire team. They had traded Drew Bledsoe to the Bills, making Tom the new face of the franchise. He was no longer battling for the starting position, but he still worked as hard as anyone in the league. He still had the same happy-go-lucky attitude that earned him the adoration of fans and the ribbing of his teammates.

With no one left to surprise, however, Tom could not just sneak up on teams in his second season as starter. The defending champions started well, winning their first three games. Tom threw for 973 yards and nine touchdowns in that span. Then, the team hit a wall. The Patriots lost four straight games. During that time, Tom threw seven interceptions, including five in the red zone. After their fourth loss, to the Broncos, Tom seemed to take out some frustration on his teammates.

"Certain guys aren't playing like it's their livelihood," Tom said.

Accusations in the media that he was blaming his teammates for the losing streak only added more pressure. Tom found himself defending his statements throughout the week. If Tom lost his fifth game in a row, the criticism would only increase, especially given New England's opponent: Drew Bledsoe and the Buffalo Bills.

Tom stepped up. He completed twenty-two of twenty-six passes for 265 yards, three touchdowns, and no interceptions. The Patriots won 38–7 and would go on to win four of their next five games. New England's season seemed to be following the template of their 2001 Cinderella run: a middling start followed by late-season momentum the team would ride into the playoffs.

That momentum came to a screeching halt in

week fourteen in Tennessee. Titans defensive end Jevon Kearse hit Tom on a pass play toward the end of the first half. The impact separated Tom's non-throwing shoulder. Ever the competitor, he ignored the pain and kept going. His play in the final three games of the season, however, was well below his usual standard. He completed just 52.73 percent of his passes and threw just two touchdowns to three interceptions.

The Patriots' final two games were against the Jets and Dolphins, the two teams with which they were vying for the division crown. After losing to New York and beating Miami, they finished 9–7 and narrowly missed the playoffs. Tom was not happy to just watch from home.

"I hate it when I turn on the TV and I have to listen to them talk about Rich Gannon or Brad Johnson," Tom told the *Boston Herald*. "I want them talking about Tom Brady. I think that's what motivates me."

The 2003 season, however, started on a down note for Tom. Five days before their first game, the Patriots cut safety Lawyer Milloy, maybe Tom's closest friend on the team. Milloy had been the player Tom had enlisted to help him turn around their 2001 season. Tom and Milloy had even filmed a cameo together in an upcoming comedy film.

To make matters worse, Milloy signed with the Buffalo Bills, the Patriots' week one opponent. New England had to start the season on the road against Milloy and Drew Bledsoe. Against his old friends, Tom had the worst game of his career. He made just fourteen of twenty-eight passes and threw four interceptions. Milloy played well. The Patriots lost 31–0. The media speculated that the Patriots—still mad about Milloy's release—would turn on their coach.

The team banded together, however, to win the next two games. In the first of those wins, against Philadelphia, Tom injured his throwing elbow when it knocked into another player's helmet. In addition to his nagging left shoulder injury, Tom would have to play with a bad right elbow all season.

It didn't seem to slow him down. After a week four loss to the Redskins, the Patriots went on a twelve-game winning streak to close out the season. Tom threw for eighteen touchdowns and just five interceptions in those games. His 85.9 passer rating for the season was not elite (he ranked tenth among quarterbacks), but was in line with his career numbers, even though he wasn't 100 percent healthy.

In the final game of the season, the Patriots got another crack at the Bills, who had humiliated them in week one. They returned the favor, beating Buffalo by the exact same 31–0 score. After the game, New England's veteran fullback Larry Centers, when asked who Tom reminded him of, paid his quarterback the ultimate compliment.

"I'd have to say Joe Montana," Centers told the *Boston Globe*. "Tom Brady is a winner. He is the best field manager I've ever seen. He plays within the scheme. He does not try to be bigger than the team."

Tom would have another chance to prove the comparison accurate. For the second time in his young career, he headed to the playoffs with home-field advantage.

CHAPTER EIGHT

★ 2004 ★

McNAIR, MANNING, AND MONTANA

Tennessee's Steve McNair and Indianapolis's Peyton Manning were co-MVPs of the 2003 NFL season. It was just the third tie in the history of the award. The two quarterbacks had plenty in common that year. They both played in the AFC South. Their teams both finished 12–4. They ranked first and second in passer rating.

They both lost to Tom Brady in the playoffs.

Despite not having the most eye-catching statistics, Tom finished third in MVP voting behind Manning and McNair. They had the numbers; Tom had the wins. Beyond that, he had the reputation of a winner, someone who did his best work in the toughest moments, when the game was in the balance. A report emerged that he had even begun telling his teammates during their winning streak, "We won't lose again."

On a January day in Massachusetts with a wind

chill that made it feel like -10 degrees outside, the Patriots' divisional round game against the Titans was a defensive affair. McNair, who had missed two of Tennessee's last three games, had a reputation of a warrior who constantly battled through injuries. But Tom was playing through pain, too. Both quarterbacks threw for just over two hundred yards and one touchdown. Then, as he did so often, Adam Vinatieri put the Patriots up, 17–14, with a late fourth-quarter field goal. The Titans couldn't answer.

New England's close win stood in stark contrast to the dominance of the Colts, their opponent in the AFC Championship game. In its first two playoff games (Indianapolis had to play in the wild card round), the Colts' offense had scored seventy-nine points. Manning had thrown for 681 total yards and eight touchdowns with no interceptions. Tom, by contrast, had totaled just 572 total yards and one touchdown during his team's entire three-game 2001 playoff run!

Tom did have one statistical advantage: his 4–0 playoff record. Manning, despite winning the first two games of these playoffs, was still just 2–3 in the postseason for his career. Broncos tight end Shannon Sharpe even dubbed Tom "Mr. January."

Still, doubts persisted about how Tom could

match up with Manning. A first-overall pick, Manning was a pedigreed former college superstar with all the physical and mental tools demanded by the position. Tom's amazing success still confounded some people.

"He's not very mobile," Broncos defensive coordinator Larry Coyer told the *Denver Post*. "And you don't think his arm is great. But, by gosh, he's a steady sucker."

That sucker was plenty steady against Coyer's defense. Just one minute and thirty seconds into his team's opening drive against the Colts, Brady called his own number on fourth and one, rushing up the middle for two yards. That gutsy call by Belichick—and his trust in Tom to convert—was rewarded a few minutes later. Seven yards from the end zone, Tom pump-faked one way before finding David Givens wide open for a touchdown. As a snow-covered New England crowd erupted, Tom let out a huge fist pump and scream in the middle of the field. Manning, meanwhile, threw two interceptions. The Patriots led 15–0 at halftime.

In the third quarter, the Colts finally scored—with a rushing touchdown. The Patriots kicked two field goals in response. Manning threw an interception. Tom answered by throwing a pick of his own. But Manning failed to capitalize, throwing his fourth intercepted pass of the day, and his third to Pats cornerback Ty Law.

Finally, with 2:30 left in the fourth quarter, Manning and the Colts' vaunted offense managed a touchdown through the air. The Colts trailed just 14–21. After Vinatieri kicked a field goal with fifty-five seconds left, Manning had one last chance to prove himself the better quarterback. He threw four straight incompletions to end the game. Afterward, the day's defensive hero, Ty Law, gave a frank assessment of the much-hyped passer matchup.

"What do stats mean when you're sitting at home?" Law said. "I want to go out there with Tom Brady. With all due respect to Steve and Peyton, winning is the card that trumps everything."

In the lead-up to Super Bowl XXXVIII in Houston, an idea began to spread: Tom Brady was the new Joe Montana. Bill Walsh, Montana's longtime coach, said as much. Even Montana himself took time to praise his longtime fan. If Tom won another Super Bowl, the parallels would be too clear to ignore. Both players had been overlooked coming out of college, only to win multiple championships. Both had proved that intelligence trumped arm strength. And most importantly, Tom and Montana had that rare ability to combine fiery competitiveness and a level head in big moments. Tom's parents were beside themselves.

"I'm awestruck by this," Tom Sr. told the San Jose *Mercury News*. "For people to mention him in the same breath as Joe Montana? For me, there's always been only one Joe Montana."

Neither quarterback in Super Bowl XXXVIII looked much like Joe Montana at first, though. For the opening twenty-six minutes of the game, neither the Patriots nor their opponents, the Carolina Panthers, scored a single point. The Pats' defense totally shut down Carolina's offense, forcing them to register negative yards. The offense, meanwhile, uncharacteristically failed to convert on two field goals.

Midway through the second quarter, with the Panthers facing third and long, New England linebacker Mike Vrabel stripped the ball from Carolina QB Jake Delhomme. On the ensuing possession, Tom faked a hand-off on the Panthers' five-yard line before finding Deion Branch up the middle for a touchdown pass. The Patriots bench celebrated. The floodgates opened.

Delhomme threw a thirty-nine-yard touchdown strike to Steve Smith two minutes later. Less than a minute after that, Brady found David Givens for a touchdown, set up by a fifty-two-yard bomb to Deion Branch. And with just twelve seconds left on the clock before halftime, the Panthers still managed to sneak in a fifty-yard field goal.

The third quarter was as quiet as the first. Then, in the final fifteen minutes of the 2003 season, the teams put on a show. The Patriots kicked off the quarter with a rushing touchdown. The Panthers answered by also running it in. Five minutes after that, with his team pinned on their own fifteen, Delhomme threw an eighty-five-yard bomb to give Carolina their first lead of the game, 22–21.

Ever cool, Tom responded by leading a methodical twelve-play, four-minute drive, capped off by a one-yard pass to Vrabel, who checked in on offense. The Patriots got the two-point conversion, but Delhomme answered with an eighty-yard drive of his own to tie it, 29–29. Once again, Tom would get the ball at the end of the Super Bowl with a chance to win it all.

The Panthers made a big mistake on the kickoff, sending the ball out of bounds. That gave Tom great field position, as he took over on his own forty with 1:08 on the clock. This time, he had all three of his time-outs. His first pass went incomplete. On second down, Carolina blitzed, but Tom hit Troy Brown, who got across midfield. Tom called a time-out. Fifty-one seconds to go.

After a play that got called back for offensive pass interference, Tom rolled left and threw a perfect thirteen-yard strike to beat double coverage and find Troy Brown. With the clock running, the Patriots hurried to the line of scrimmage. Tom found tight end Daniel Graham underneath for a four-yard pickup. With fifteen seconds, New England used another time-out.

On third and three on Carolina's forty-yard line, they were not in prime position for a Vinatieri field goal. They needed another ten yards or so to give their kicker a chance. Tom got him seventeen, hitting Deion Branch on the right sideline. The Pats called their final time-out with nine seconds left in the game. Tom had done it again, playing methodically on football's stage—late in the fourth quarter of the Super Bowl—to give his team a chance to win.

The kick team set up. Vinatieri had missed one from thirty-one yards out earlier in the game, and had a thirty-six yarder blocked. This one would be forty-one yards. He lined up. Carolina called a timeout. Vinatieri reset. The center snapped the ball. The hold was clean. The kick went up. Good!

The Patriots had won their fifteenth game in a row and their second championship in three years. At just twenty-six, Tom won his second Super Bowl MVP award. In doing so, he joined an elite group of players to have won two or more: Bart Starr, Terry Bradshaw, and . . . Joe Montana.

Suddenly the Patriots were a budding dynasty, and Tom their superstar leader.

CHAPTER NINE

★ 2004 ★

REPEAT

On October 31, 2004, the unthinkable happened: the New England Patriots lost a football game. The Steelers defeated the Pats 20–34, in Pittsburgh. It was the team's first loss since September 28...of the prior year. Tom had led his team to twenty-one straight victories (including the three playoff wins from earlier in the year). It is still an NFL record.

All that winning had made Tom Brady famous... really famous. Before the previous season's Super Bowl, he attended the State of the Union address as a guest of First Lady Laura Bush. The former altar boy from San Mateo met Pope St. John Paul II. He even appeared in an episode of *The Simpsons*.

Tom did not let that fame go to his head, nor did he forget where he came from. He donated the car he won as Super Bowl XXXVIII MVP to Junípero Serra High School, where it was raffled off to raise money for the school. He also moved to downtown

Boston, hoping he'd have better luck blending into the crowds and not sticking out.

On the field, he stayed extremely focused, as evidenced by the Patriots' 6–0 record going into that week eight loss to the Steelers. The Patriots' offense in 2004 benefited from the acquisition of veteran running back Corey Dillon in the off-season. Dillon would rush for 1,635 yards in fifteen games that season, a New England franchise record that still stands.

Dillon's arrival took pressure off Tom, allowing him to play his usual mistake-free, managerial style of quarterback. Still, that dynamic led to people outside the organization questioning Tom's place among the league's best quarterbacks. The 2004 season featured some all-time great quarterbacking performances, led by Indianapolis's Peyton Manning. The Colts signal caller had a 121.1 passer rating and set the single-season touchdown record with forty-nine. Tom noticed but stayed focused on team success.

"I look around at the other quarterbacks in the league, too. I'm like, 'That guy is throwing for this? And this guy is throwing for that?' " Tom told the

Boston Herald. "But would I trade that for a lesser record than we have? Certainly not."

Patriots head coach Bill Belichick gave a more succinct answer: "In Tom's case, his rating isn't stats but wins." And Tom had plenty of those. The Patriots finished 14–2 again, despite sometimes inconsistent play by Tom. As his completion percentage dipped below 60 percent, at times, and questions arose about his accuracy, Tom would respond with an amazing play—like a pass he made while sitting down in week thirteen against Cincinnati—or a forward-looking sound bite.

"On to the Jets," Tom said after he threw four interceptions in one of his worst games ever, against the Dolphins. "Who wants to talk about that?"

That single-minded focus on the next game was the most important trait of the Patriots' budding dynasty. Coach Belichick tailored the game plan to each opponent. And New England's players always focused on the task at hand, instead of dwelling on the week before. That mentality carried them back to home-field advantage in the divisional round of the playoffs, where they would meet a familiar foe: Manning's Colts.

Manning may have had the greatest regular season of all time, but in the playoffs—and in Foxborough—he still had plenty to prove. He was 0–5 all time against Tom and 0–6 on the road against the Patriots. Tom meanwhile had a streak of his own on the line: he had won his first six playoff games. Still, the matchup led to the inevitable comparisons between the two quarterbacks, and the question as to whether Tom was merely the product of a great system.

Well, the system worked. The game conditions were bad for offense—muddy, snowy, and windy. The Patriots' defense took advantage, holding the Colts to just a field goal all day. Manning fumbled the ball and threw a pick on their final drive. Tom, as always, won out with mistake-free football. The Patriots won 20–3. Once again, Peyton Manning would be the best quarterback watching Tom from home.

Next up were the Steelers in Pittsburgh, the place where the Patriots' twenty-one-game winning streak had ended in week eight. Steelers rookie quarterback Ben Roethlisberger had gone 13–0 during the regular season. He was, in many ways, the opposite of Tom Brady: highly touted out of college, a tremendous athlete, and a player who did his best work when the play broke down. The Steelers also boasted the league's number-one defense, in contrast to the Colts, who had ranked twenty-ninth in yards allowed.

Playing the NFL's most fearsome defense would have been enough for Tom to deal with. But the night before the game, he found himself battling a 103-degree fever. Unlike during their first Super Bowl run in 2001, the Pats couldn't just send out Drew Bledsoe for the AFC Championship game and get Tom back for the Super Bowl. So the Patriots starter took the field in 11-degree weather the next day in Pittsburgh.

No one would have known Tom was sick—not how he was playing. On just his second pass attempt of the game, he faked the hand-off and found Deion Branch deep for a sixty-yard touchdown. He would follow that up with another forty-five-yard strike to Branch in the second quarter, which set up a nine-yard passing touchdown to David Givens.

Roethlisberger, meanwhile, threw a touchdown of his own—to the wrong team. After Tom's second touchdown, Pittsburgh's passer made a rookie mistake by staring right at his intended target. Pats safety Rodney Harrison jumped the route and ran the ball eighty-seven yards for a touchdown. The Patriots led 24–3 at halftime and held on to win 41–27. The Patriots got their revenge, feverish quarterback and all, and were headed back to the Super Bowl.

This time around, Tom Brady was not going to surprise anyone. Unlike in past years, when opponents had downplayed Tom's importance to the Patriots, he had the respect of the Eagles, his opponent in Super Bowl XXXIX.

"He's six five and it seems like he's six nine back there," legendary Eagles defensive coordinator Jim Johnson was quoted saying in the *New York Post*. "Nothing bothers him, that's probably the most impressive thing. He's playing at a high level, but the biggest thing is how big he looks back there."

Tom took the field at Alltel Stadium in Jacksonville, Florida, with a heavy heart. Earlier in that week, his ninety-four-year-old grandmother Margaret "Peggy" Brady had died. Peggy, who had collected newspaper clippings about her famous grandson, would sit on game days and pray for Tom's health while the family in San Mateo called her with updates.

Much like in last year's championship game, Super Bowl XXXIX got off to a slow start. The Patriots' inability to take advantage of Philly turnovers kept the game scoreless until Eagles QB Donovan McNabb threw a touchdown pass in the second quarter. On the following drive, the Patriots seemed poised to tie it with the ball on Philadelphia's four-yard line. Tom called for a play-action pass, on which he would fake a hand-off to running back Kevin Faulk. He left the ball out too far. Faulk ran into it and knocked it out of Tom's hand. The Eagles recovered.

But McNabb failed to capitalize on Tom's mistake. So before halftime, the Patriots had one more chance. Tom calmly drove his team all the way back to Philadelphia's four. He dropped back to pass and scanned his options. Tight end Christian Fauria, the primary receiver, slipped and fell. Deion Branch was double-covered. But he didn't panic and kept going through his progressions. He found David Givens, who had quietly snuck to the sideline in the right side of the end zone. Touchdown! The game was tied, 7–7.

Tom followed that up with a touchdown to linebacker Mike Vrabel on the opening drive of the third quarter. (It was the second year in a row the defensive standout caught an offensive touchdown for the Pats in the Super Bowl.) McNabb answered seven and a half minutes later, marching the Eagles down the field for a touchdown-scoring drive of their own.

Tom never flinched. He went four-for-four on the next drive, before Corey Dillon punched it in with a two-yard run at the start of the fourth quarter. 21–14. After the Eagles went three-and-out on their next possession, Tom and Branch hooked up on an impossible pass. Running across the middle of the field, Branch jumped over an Eagles player, and Tom threw the ball right above the fingertips of the covering defender. That set up a Vinatieri field goal: 24–14. This time, the Pats wouldn't need a last-minute game-winning drive.

That burden fell on the Eagles, who scored a touchdown with 1:55 on the clock—to cut the lead to three—and then got the ball back at their four with forty-six seconds left. Philadelphia's two-minute offense stood in stark contrast to the Pats. McNabb advanced the ball nowhere in two plays and took twenty-nine seconds off the clock in the process. Rodney Harrison intercepted a desperate Hail Mary pass with nine seconds left.

For the first time in his Super Bowl career, Tom could take a knee on the final play. Tom and the Patriots joined Troy Aikman and the early '90s Cowboys as the only teams to win three out of four consecutive Super Bowls. It seemed like Tom Brady just couldn't lose in the playoffs.

CHAPTER TEN

★ 2005–2006 ★

SHOULDERING THE LOAD

The more successful Tom and the Patriots were, the harder winning was going to get. For one thing, everyone else in the league wanted a piece of them. If winning the Super Bowl hadn't put enough of a target on their backs, winning two consecutive Super Bowls certainly did that. They also faced the same problems all sports dynasties encounter. The more an organization wins, the more other teams will want its players and coaches—and the harder it will be for the successful franchise to retain those personnel.

Before the 2005 season, Tom Brady lost his offensive coordinator, Charlie Weis, who accepted the head-coaching job at the University of Notre Dame, and wide receiver David Patten, who signed as a free agent with the Washington Redskins. The Patriots also said good-bye to defensive coordinator Romeo Crennel, who became the head coach of the Cleveland Browns.

Belichick did not name a replacement for Weis.

Play-calling duties would be split among several coaches, including quarterbacks coach Josh McDaniels, who was twenty-nine, just one year older than Tom. Without a veteran coach to lean on, Tom had to step up. He also had to live up to the six-year, $60-million contract he signed over the off-season. He likely could have demanded much more, but, as always, prioritized winning and the success of the Patriots as an organization.

"Is it going to make me feel any better to make an extra million?" he said to *Sports Illustrated*. "That million might be more important to the team."

Amid all these changes and in spite of his successes, Tom maintained his legendary competitive drive. One newspaper story out of training camp reported that he slammed his helmet on the ground and brooded on the sideline after a single bad pass. Belichick had to order him to take days off.

When the season started, the Patriots lost more key figures from their Super Bowl run—this time to injuries. Safety Rodney Harrison would play just three games all season. Running back Corey Dillon missed four games and his backup, Kevin Faulk, went down at the same time.

With Dillon unable to repeat his 2004, Tom

picked up the slack, throwing for over 4,000 yards (4,110) for the first time in his career. His completion percentage also jumped to 63.0 percent, up from 60.8 percent the year before. The key stat for Tom had always been wins, however, and this season they didn't come as easily.

The surest sign that things had changed came in week nine, when Peyton Manning came to Foxborough and finally won. Manning and Tom both threw for three touchdowns, but the Colts won, 40–21. The Patriots' defense, a cornerstone of their dynasty, had slipped. In 2005, it would allow the seventh-most yards in the league. The Colts left New England 8–0 and Super Bowl favorites. The Pats dropped to 4–4.

Losing obviously frustrated Tom. After a week four loss to the Chargers, San Diego coach Marty Schottenheimer commented on the key players the Patriots were missing. His remarks could hardly be construed as criticism, but Tom lashed out, telling the *Boston Herald,* "You don't talk about our team. He has no business talking about our team."

As if in the final drive of a Super Bowl, Tom refused to let the Pats fade away. After the team fell to 6–5 following a week twelve loss to the Chiefs, they rallied for four straight wins, taking advantage of two games against their lowly division rival, the New York Jets. Tom had a 100.3 passer rating in those games. The Patriots were going to the playoffs after all, but Tom would have two new postseason experiences.

The first new experience was a game in the wild-card round. The Patriots had become accustomed to a first-round bye and home-field advantage in the second round. This time, they got neither.

The 12–4 Jacksonville Jaguars traveled far from sunny Florida to play the Pats in their wild-card game in Massachusetts. Like with so many teams, their offense froze in the cold. The Patriots won 28–3 behind three touchdown passes from Tom. Suddenly, the defending champs looked like just that. The dream of a "three-peat" seemed real again.

Then, one week later, in Denver, Tom would have that other new experience: he would lose a playoff game. After an interception and a missed field goal, the Patriots found themselves in a fourth-quarter hole against the Broncos that not even the Comeback Kid could climb out of: down 24–6 with under nine minutes left. Tom got New England within eleven with a touchdown, but Denver responded with a field goal to stretch the lead to fourteen.

On his final drive of the season, Tom did not set up

a field goal or kneel as the Broncos celebration began. He threw . . . an interception. He was human after all, 10–1 in career playoff games. Later, the team would reveal that Tom had played the entire second half of the season—New England's best stretch—with a hernia that required off-season surgery.

DYNASTY DIES IN DENVER read one newspaper headline. Announced another, DYNASTY CRUMBLES.

Those headlines would eventually prove wrong. Before the 2006 season, however, it was clear things would get harder for Tom before they got easier. After losing David Patten the year before, Tom had to say good-bye to his top two wideouts. David Givens, who had caught fifty-nine passes for 739 yards, signed with Tennessee. Then the Patriots traded Deion Branch (998 yards and five touchdowns) to the Seattle Seahawks for a first-round pick. The Patriots also parted with longtime kicker Adam Vinatieri, who left for Indianapolis.

The Patriots rebounded in 2006, finishing 12–4. The improvement had much to do with their defense, which allowed the second-fewest points in the league. On offense, the team ran the ball better, behind the duo of Dillon and rookie Laurence Maroney. But Tom clearly felt the effect of a depleted receiving corps, throwing for the fewest passing yards (3,529) in any full season in his career.

But individual statistics had never been Tom's focus—or why he had become so popular in the first place. The Pats were back in the playoffs. There, the old Tom Brady magic seemed to be back. They trounced their division rival Jets in the wild-card round, 37–16. Then they went to San Diego to face a Chargers team picked by many to win the Super Bowl.

And in a near mirror of the previous year's situation in Denver, the Patriots found themselves down with less than nine minutes to go. This time, however, the Patriots only needed eight points to tie. And they had luck on their side, as a potential game-sealing interception on fourth down was fumbled by Chargers safety Marlon McCree. Tom capitalized on the mistake and finished the drive with a touchdown pass and a two-point conversion.

After a three-and-out from the Chargers, Tom took over on his own fifteen-yard line and led another long scoring drive, this time capped off by a field goal by Stephen Gostkowski, Vinatieri's replacement. Tom had pulled off another amazing comeback. The Pats had just one hurdle left to return to the Super Bowl: Peyton Manning.

Manning still put up gaudier statistics than Tom in the regular season. Only now, he beat Tom on the field, too. He followed up 2005's win in Foxborough with another in 2006. Those games, however, had come in the regular season. Manning had still never beaten Tom in the playoffs and had never won the Super Bowl. At least this time, Tom would be in Peyton's house: the RCA Dome in Indianapolis.

The game started typically. The Patriots scored on a Colts fumble. Corey Dillon scored on a seven-yard run. And Manning threw a pick-six to Asante Samuel. Suddenly, at halftime, the Patriots led 21–6. The old dynamic seemed intact: Manning won regular season awards; Tom won big games.

Then in the second half, Manning took over. He led a fourteen-play drive that ended with him sneaking the ball across the goal line himself to start the third quarter. After a three-and-out from New England, Manning did it again, and threw for the two-point conversion. Suddenly, in eleven minutes, the Patriots lead had evaporated. The score was 21–21.

Tom answered with a touchdown pass. The Colts rushed for one. 28–28. In the fourth quarter, the teams went back and forth kicking field goals and the Patriots hopped back on top, 34–31. Then, starting on his own twenty and with 2:17 on the clock, Manning led a touchdown drive. His only mistake: he scored too quickly. With about a minute left on the clock and two time-outs, the Comeback Kid had everything he needed. Sitting on the bench, Manning couldn't bring himself to watch.

Tom hit tight end Ben Watson for nineteen yards. Then he found fullback Heath Evans for fifteen. The Patriots called a time-out with twenty-four seconds and forty-five yards from Super Bowl XLI. Tom dropped back. He felt pressure on his left. He threw to Watson. Intercepted.

Manning finally beat Tom in the playoffs, and then triumphed over the Bears in the Super Bowl. Suddenly, the conversation about the league's best quarterback had left Tom Brady behind. That wouldn't last for long.

CHAPTER ELEVEN

★ 2007 ★

ALMOST PERFECT

"Everybody knows who I am," said wide receiver Randy Moss when asked if he thought arriving at New England was a chance to revive his career. "I don't need to revitalize nothing."

Quarterbacks are not alone out there. No position in sports is more singularly responsible for team success than the passer. Ironically, no position requires more support.

Entire careers of once-promising signal callers have been squandered because their teams did not protect them from oncoming pass rushes with solid offensive lines. Maybe their coaches never surrounded them with receivers who could catch the ball or running backs who could keep opposing defenses honest.

Tom Brady was the biggest start of the most successful NFL franchise of the '00s. He had already led his team to three Super Bowl victories—more than most Hall of Famers did in their entire careers.

Still, he lacked the trophy case of an elite passer. He had never been named All-Pro and had only made the Pro Bowl in three out of six seasons as a starter. He had never been named league MVP.

Perhaps not coincidentally, Tom had never played with a true number-one wide receiver in an era rife with them. Players like Terrell Owens, Chad Johnson, Torry Holt, Andre Johnson, Marvin Harrison, and Reggie Wayne all regularly enjoyed 1,000-yard seasons. For five seasons after Tom's first year as a starter, the Pats did not boast a single 1,000-yard receiver. In 2006, Reche Caldwell led all Patriots in the category with just 760 yards.

That was not going to be the case in 2007. Belichick spent the off-season finding a whole new corps of wideouts for Tom, including Moss, who was coming off a disappointing season in which he had just 553 yards receiving in thirteen games with the Raiders. That's why he was asked if coming to New England could revitalize his career. But his answer was correct: he didn't need to prove anything. He was already one of the greatest wide receivers of all time, having eclipsed ten thousand yards and one hundred touchdowns before his age-thirty season.

Moss, a lanky six four, was the perfect wide receiver. Unlike Tom, who did not have all the physical tools scouts sought when he came out of college, Moss broke the mold. He was tall, fast, and had great leaping ability. Those gifts, combined with his route running, "football IQ," and tremendous hands, gave him the ability to make any catch in any kind of coverage. After his poor season on a disastrous Oakland team, Belichick acquired him for just a fourth-round pick.

The Patriots coach made another shrewd trade when he acquired receiver and punt returner Wes Welker from the Miami Dolphins for a second- and a seventh-round pick. Welker had a solid season with Miami in 2006, catching sixty-seven passes for 687 yards. Additionally, the team signed Donté Stallworth, who had 725 yards with the Eagles.

The most significant off-season acquisition for Tom, however, was even shorter than the five foot nine inches Welker. On August 22, 2007, Tom's first son, John "Jack" Edward Thomas Moynahan was born in LA to Tom's ex-girlfriend, actress Bridget Moynahan.

Not long after Jack's birth, his dad was back on

the field for the Pats' September 9, week one matchup with the New York Jets. Instantly, everything seemed different. These Patriots were not the scrappy well-coached bunch that had won three Super Bowls. They, and Tom specifically, had become something more.

On the opening drive of the season, Tom found Welker for nine yards, then ten yards, then an eleven-yard score. The short and elusive receiver would line up in the slot and become a nightmare for opposing defenses all season, drawing players simply not fast enough to cover him.

Randy Moss created an entirely different problem for other teams. At the start of the third quarter, with New England already up 21–7 over New York, Tom dropped back on a play-action pass near midfield. He sat back in the pocket with plenty of time and hopped forward, loading up for a big throw. When he finally uncorked the pass, Moss was outracing three Jets defenders to the goal line, where he caught the ball in stride and glided in to score. Suddenly, a quarterback who had lacked weapons just a season ago now could throw to the league's best slot receiver and deep threat.

The Patriots beat the Jets 38–14 and quickly proved that blowout was no fluke. Tom threw for at least three touchdowns in the first five games of the season. Then in week six against the Cowboys, he threw five. As an encore, in week seven against the Dolphins, he threw *six*, one shy of tying the NFL record. In that game he threw two to Welker, two to Moss, one to Stallworth, and one to tight end Kyle Brady (no relation).

The Patriots' offense wasn't just improved. It was historically good. That set up an exciting week nine rematch of the AFC Championship game. In Indianapolis, the Colts and Pats would face off, both undefeated, both boasting potent passing attacks.

New England's juggernaut offense stalled. Tom threw one touchdown and two interceptions and found himself down 20–10 with less than ten minutes to go. Yet again, he found himself needing to lead a comeback against the Colts. Things had changed since the final minute of last year's playoffs. Tom now had Randy Moss.

On second and ten from his own forty-two, Tom dropped back in the shotgun. While the CBS announcers on the broadcast talked about how well the Colts defended the deep ball, Tom stood tall in the pocket and threw a high, arcing pass, as if he wanted to hit the roof of the RCA Dome. The ball found Randy Moss on the Colts' three-yard line, where he caught the ball against his body despite pass interference from the defending safety. The drive finished with Welker tap-dancing past the pylon for the score. 20–17.

After the Colts punted on the ensuing drive, Tom again went deep from midfield, this time finding Donté Stallworth for a thirty-three-yard strike along the left sideline. He followed it up with a thirteen-yard touchdown pass to running back Kevin Faulk. The Patriots stayed perfect.

"The thing is, we're 9–0 and it really doesn't matter," said Tom. "It just doesn't matter. None of this matters. What matters is January. That's what matters."

While Tom may have focused on getting back to the Super Bowl, fans and the media loved New England's chase of the 1972 Dolphins, the only undefeated team in NFL history. And the MVP debate, for once, did not involve Peyton Manning. The Patriots had two serious contenders for the award: Tom Brady and Randy Moss.

Moss and Tom were not rivals, however. Tom requested specifically before the season that they have lockers right next to each other. That way, they could become closer on and off the field. Both players recognized a once-in-a-lifetime opportunity. They were arguably the two greatest players ever at their respective positions. Moss matched Tom's legendary work ethic as they constantly went over plays and situations together. He affectionately referred to his quarterback as "Tommy boy."

That bond became obvious late in the season when ESPN analyst Ron Jaworski accused Moss of loafing during the Pats' close 31–28 week twelve win over the Eagles. Tom denied that his favorite target had taken a play off all season.

"We got each other's back," Moss said. "I've been hated all my life, and I don't think it's going to stop now. When you're up, people hate you. When you're down, they love you."

Love them or hate them, Brady and Moss entered the final game of the regular season ready to make history. Set to play the Giants in New York, Tom sat at forty-eight touchdowns, one fewer than the record set by Peyton Manning in 2004, while Moss had twenty-one, one fewer than Jerry Rice's receiving record from 1987. The Patriots as a team were

15–0, on the precipice of becoming the only team to go undefeated in the modern sixteen-game schedule.

On the opening play of the second quarter, down four points, Tom took a snap four yards from New York's end zone. Moss was covered, so Tom threw it high, where only he could leap and catch it. He held onto the ball going to the ground, somersaulting over his defender. Touchdown! With the score, the Patriots passed the 1998 Vikings—another team with Randy Moss—for the most points in an NFL season (560). The passing and receiving TD records were tied.

The game was back-and-forth. The Patriots found themselves down 23–28 in the fourth quarter. On second and ten, Tom was on his own thirty-five. The guy covering Moss fell. But Tom underthrew his wide-open target. Tom wasn't content to just throw for the first down on the next play, however. He threw deep down the right sideline, where Moss had simply outraced the defender. He sprinted to the end zone. Touchdown number fifty!

The Pats won, 38–35, completing the undefeated season. Tom, who had preached all season that only the playoffs mattered, allowed himself to celebrate the feat after the game. Even the ever-stoic coach Belichick said it was "a great feeling."

"We've been dealing with being undefeated all season," Tom said. "It was kind of a strange game. It really doesn't mean much to either team, but it means a lot."

The game didn't "mean much to either team," because they were both already in the playoffs. In fact, the Giants and Patriots would meet in that season's Super Bowl. The Patriots had cruised to the Super Bowl with two decisive wins, while the Giants had gutted out three road wins, including in overtime against the Packers in the NFC Championship game.

But at Super Bowl XLII in Arizona, the pressure was all on the Patriots. If they won this game, they would be the undisputed greatest football team of all time—and Tom the greatest quarterback.

Whether or not the always-cool Tom Brady felt any of the pressure of winning the biggest game of his life, he certainly felt a very different kind of pressure coming from all sides of the Patriots' collapsing pocket. The Giants' defense had led the league with fifty-three sacks during the regular season—the Patriots had ranked second with forty-seven. In the

Super Bowl, both teams got to the quarterback, with the Giants sacking Tom five times.

That defensive battle led to a 7–3 score until early in the fourth quarter, when Giants quarterback Eli Manning threw for a touchdown to give his team a 10–7 lead. Tom responded, as he had so many times in big playoff games, with a long, methodical march to the end zone. He threw three passes to Welker and three to Moss, including a six-yard touchdown. 14–10.

Manning would likely have just one chance to answer. With just 1:15 left on the clock, he faced a key third and five from his own forty-four. Manning dropped back. The pocket collapsed, and multiple Patriots pulled on his jersey but were unable to get him down. Manning rolled out of the pocket and threw a deep wobbly pass. A Giants receiver caught the ball, despite tight coverage, by pinning it against his helmet as he fell to the ground.

The play was a sports miracle, and it allowed the Giants to go twenty-four more yards to score. After yet another sack on first down, Tom would have just twenty-five seconds to get from his own sixteen-yard line into field goal range. The Giants players looked nervous on the bench. The Patriots had the most explosive offense of all time.

Tom rolled right and loaded up for a big throw. The ball sailed sixty-four yards, where Randy Moss was in double coverage. The throw was right on line, but a defender deflected it away at the last moment. Fourth down. Tom tried again. Incomplete.

The Patriots' perfect season had been undone by the most unlikely play in the history of the Super Bowl. Tom marched off the field with helmet in hand and his head hanging. Still, Tom had proven what he could do with a more talented group of receivers. The player many doubted could even become a pro quarterback had staked his claim as the greatest player in the history of the sport.

CHAPTER TWELVE

★ 2008–2009 ★

INJURY AND COMEBACK

Tom Brady's next attempt at a perfect season would last only seven minutes. Midway through the first quarter of the first game of 2008, he fell awkwardly when a Kansas City Chief's pass rusher grabbed his leg. He writhed on the field in pain, clutching his left knee. Eventually, he limped off the field with the help of two Patriots trainers.

The next day, Bill Belichick announced that Tom would miss the entire 2008 season. He had torn his anterior cruciate ligament and medial collateral ligament. Tom, who had played 128 straight games, had never suffered a major football injury before. He had surgery in California and then returned to Boston for rehabilitation. While he could not help them on the field, Tom's presence and upbeat attitude still inspired his teammates.

"It's just good to hear his voice," running back BenJarvus Green-Ellis told the *Boston Globe*.

Tom's backup, Matt Cassel, played well and led

the team to an 11–5 record. Still, New England missed the playoffs in an unusually strong AFC field. And while his buddies battled on the field, Tom kept busy. On February 26, 2009, he married his girlfriend of two years, Brazilian model Gisele Bündchen, at a ceremony in Santa Monica, California. Having the wedding in California made it easier for Tom's son, Jack, to attend—the two got to spend more time together all year with a less intense football schedule for Dad. Tom's rehabilitation was even slightly set back when he developed an infection after playing with Jack two days after his operation, against the wishes of his doctors.

Being away from the field also gave Tom time to reflect on his career. Though Tom had to work as hard as anyone in the game to prove himself an NFL starter and then one of the all-time great quarterbacks, he had never had a real down year that made him question his commitment to the sport or his long-term goals. Success had come quickly for him, with three championships in his first four seasons. Sitting at home, Tom realized one thing: he loved football and wanted to keep playing for a long time.

"The reality is, in this sport, you really never know," Tom said during his rehabilitation. "Any day could be your last day in football. I don't think about the end too often. Hopefully this is still, relatively, in the early part of my career."

Tom referred to the injury and recovery as "half-time" for his career. Next season would be his tenth in the NFL. He wanted to play at least another ten after that—until he was forty-one. It was an ambitious goal, but doubting Tom Brady hadn't worked out for anyone before.

The second half of Tom's career picked up where the first half left off. Tom threw for 378 yards and two touchdowns in week one of the 2009 season, against the Bills. Tom did not throw for fifty touchdowns in 2009 like he had in 2007. He finished the season with 4,398 yards passing and twenty-eight touchdowns. Still, he posted the second-best passer rating (96.2) of his career, proving that 2007 had been no fluke, and the injury was not going to slow him down.

In the last game of the season, against the Texans, Wes Welker suffered the same knee injury Tom had. He had caught a league-leading 123 passes during the season—16 more than the next best receiver. So the 10–6 Patriots entered the playoffs without Tom's favorite target. Tom was also believed to have broken ribs and a broken finger, though he wouldn't admit to either injury, pointing out that lots of people played hurt.

In the wild-card round, they welcomed the Baltimore Ravens to Foxborough. Despite everything Tom and his teammates had been through the last few years, they had still never lost a playoff game at home and were undefeated at Gillette Stadium that season. That made it only more surprising when the Ravens went up 14–0 five minutes into the game. They ran eighty-three yards straight up the middle to score on the first play of the game. Then, on their next drive, they handed it off five more times and scored.

The Pats couldn't stop the run—Baltimore QB Joe Flacco only completed four passes all day, but his team won 33–14. Tom had the worst playoff game of his career, averaging just 3.67 yards per pass attempt and throwing three interceptions. The Pats fans booed the team that had given them so much.

"I'd have been booing us, too, the way we played," Tom said after the game. "Playing the way we played today, we weren't going to beat anybody."

After getting blown out at home, the media began to speculate the Patriots' dynasty had ended. Never before had they seemed so ill prepared for a game, much less a playoff game at home. Tom would be entering his midthirties soon. Besides, New England had been the team of the 2000s. It was a new decade.

But Tom didn't buy it.

"We have Mr. Kraft and Coach Belichick, who is probably the greatest coach of all time and a great core leader," he said. "We have a lot of youth that are really good players and work hard. I certainly don't think just because we lose a couple of games this year that all of a sudden everything's over."

Of course, nothing was over for Tom Brady and the Pats. The second half of his career was going to be better than the first—and it was just beginning.

CHAPTER THIRTEEN

★ 2010–2011 ★

BENNY AND THE JETS

"I hate the Jets," Tom Brady said on Boston radio before the 2010 season. "I refuse to support that show."

The show in question was *Hard Knocks*, a documentary series about the Patriots rivals, the New York Jets. Many expected the Jets—under second-year coach Rex Ryan and second-year quarterback Mark Sanchez—to challenge the Patriots in the AFC East. Through his colorful quips on the show, Ryan had made the Jets popular. And he made it known that he shared Tom's feelings about the rivalry.

"My brother got a couple Super Bowl rings," Ryan said, referring to twin Rob, who had coached linebackers during the Patriots' first two Super Bowl wins. "He loves Tom Brady, but I don't have them, so I don't like Tom Brady. I respect him, but I don't like him."

Tom's comment about hating the Jets made headlines precisely because the quarterback so rarely spoke out to the media. The Pats, like their quarterback and their coach, quietly went about their business and won. Those two things made opposing fans view them as villains. The outspoken and goofy Jets were a perfect foil.

Sharpening the contrast were stories coming out of training camp of Tom getting on his teammates for their mistakes. The veteran QB, however, was just making sure that his young receiving corps could handle one of the league's most complex offenses. Wes Welker was likely to miss time recovering from his knee injury. And the Patriots would trade an aging Randy Moss after just four games. Tom would need to rely on players like rookie tight end Rob Gronkowski.

"Gronk," a second-round pick out of Arizona, was an unprecedented talent at his position. Six foot six and as strong as a defensive lineman, Gronkowski ran and caught like a wide receiver. He gave the Pats a unique red zone weapon: Gronk logged ten touchdowns in his rookie season despite having just forty-two total catches.

Then, of course, there was a youngster Tom was most excited to welcome to his team: his new son, Benjamin Brady, born December 8, 2009. Tom's play had improved, maybe coincidentally, after his first son was born. With two kids, he was ready for another historic season.

But first, the Jets-Patriots rivalry would get more fuel. New England would visit New York for week two. But even after a win at home in their first game, against the Bengals, Tom was talking about the Jets.

"The road environment is very different than our friendly home crowd who, when I looked up, half the stadium was gone when we were up twenty-one points in the early fourth quarter, which I wasn't so happy about," he said. "I don't think the Jets fans leave early. They're going to be loud the whole game."

They had reason to be loud. The Jets beat the Patriots 28–14. Afterward, the Jets players and coach talked about what a monumental win it was for their team. Tom and the Pats went back to work.

By week thirteen, the Jets and Pats were both 9–2. They met to play their second game of the season in Gillette Stadium. It was perhaps the most anticipated game of the NFL regular season. But the Patriots won easily, 45–3. Tom threw for four touchdowns and a near-perfect 148.9 passer rating. He hated the Jets, and now they had even more reason to hate him, too.

The Jets weren't getting special treatment, however. The Patriots won their final four games of the season by a margin of 184–47. Tom finished the season with thirty-six touchdowns to just four interceptions, and a 111.0 passer rating. Statistically, he had nearly matched his historic 2007 campaign, and all while shepherding a young group of receivers. He was unanimously voted the NFL's Most Valuable Player.

Also like in 2007, a great regular season preceded a disappointing postseason. In the divisional round, the Patriots welcomed the Jets back to New England. New York remembered the lessons of their humiliating week thirteen loss. Tom played well, but so did his opposite on the Jets, Sanchez, who threw three touchdowns en route to a 28–21 win.

The preseason narrative had been that the Patriots were in decline and the Jets were coming to take their spot. This playoff win seemingly confirmed it. But New York would go on to lose in the AFC Championship game to the Steelers. Sanchez would last just three more seasons in New York, Ryan four. Though it was just the first year of the 2010s, that playoff win would be the high point of the Jets' decade—another decade that would be dominated by Tom Brady and the Patriots.

CHAPTER FOURTEEN

★ 2011 ★

YEAR OF THE QUARTERBACK

Another year meant another New York quarterback to challenge Tom. In a radio interview in New York, Giants quarterback Eli Manning, who had beaten Tom in Super Bowl XLII, claimed he was in the same class as New England's QB. The statement raised some eyebrows—while Tom had been last season's unanimous MVP, Manning had led the league in interceptions, with twenty-five. Before the season was over, though, the Giants signal caller would get a chance to prove his point.

Before the 2011 season, ESPN would declare it the "Year of the Quarterback," as they rolled out a spate of programming related to the NFL's most glamorous position. Tom even got his own documentary, *The Brady 6,* about the six quarterbacks selected before Tom in the 2000 draft. All six of them were out of football by 2011—most never made it in the first place. At age thirty-four, Tom had outlasted them all.

ESPN's declaration turned out to be more right than they could have known. Despite Eli's big brother Peyton missing the entire season with a neck injury, quarterback play was never better. Tom eclipsed Dan Marino's single-season record of 5,084 passing yards with 5,235. But New Orleans' Drew Brees eclipsed him, finishing the season with 5,476. Brees and Green Bay's Aaron Rodgers also challenged Tom's single-season touchdown record, finishing with forty-six and forty-five, respectively.

For Tom—a player always more focused on the team than himself—it was not the Year of the Quarterback but a year to settle old scores. The Patriots had not been back to the Super Bowl in four years. Even more frustrating for Tom, they had not won one in seven years.

"There's only one team every year that has a good season, and we haven't been that team in a long time," Tom said.

So Tom took aim at everyone that had stood between him and his one goal in recent memory. First: the New York Jets. The Patriots beat their division rival twice in 2011, first 30–21 in week five and then in a 37–16 blowout in week ten. Entering that second game, both teams had been 5–3. It was yet another opportunity for one team to seize control of the AFC East. The Patriots took it and never looked back.

Beating the Jets was a turning point in New England's season. They closed out the regular season by winning their final seven games. That gave Tom a shot in the postseason against the Denver Broncos, the team that gave him his first playoff loss. Led by second-year quarterback and college football legend Tim Tebow, the Broncos had pulled off a miraculous comeback in their wild-card round win over the Pittsburgh Steelers.

In Foxborough, though, Denver's carriage turned into a pumpkin. An overmatched Tebow completed just nine passes, while Tom threw for six touchdowns. The Patriots won the game 45–10. Next up on Tom Brady's revenge tour: the Baltimore Ravens, the team that had beaten him in the playoffs at home for the first time.

The Ravens put up a better fight than the Broncos. Though the Patriots led 16–10 at one point in the third quarter, Baltimore went ahead late on a twenty-nine-yard touchdown pass from quarterback Joe Flacco. After the Pats fumbled the following kickoff, the Ravens drove downfield again and kicked a field goal to take a 20–16 lead.

With the ball finally back in his hands, Tom wasted no time getting the Patriots in Ravens territory, hitting Gronkowski for a twenty-three-yard strike down the field. After a series of short plays, Tom got his team to the Ravens' one-yard line with just over twelve minutes to go. On second and goal, Tom called his own number, rushing left for the end zone. Touchdown! But wait... instant replay showed Tom's knee down before the ball crossed the plane. The score remained. On the next play, Pats running back BenJarvus Green-Ellis tried to leap over the line to get that last yard, only to be met by Ravens linebacker Ray Lewis.

Fourth down. The Patriots could have kicked an easy field goal to cut the Ravens' lead to one with plenty of time left on the clock and set up a potential game-winning field goal later. Belichick, however, sent his offense back on the field, not the kick team. And where his twenty-six-year-old running back failed, his thirty-four-year-old quarterback would succeed. Tom took the snap and leaped over the center, reaching the ball out across the plane. The player who had tested poorly in the vertical jump at the combine more than a decade ago had just jumped over an entire offensive line, and in the process, maybe sent his team back to the Super Bowl.

With fifteen seconds left in the game, the Ravens would get a chance to tie the game with a thirty-two-yard field goal. The kick went up . . . and sailed wide left!

Tom Brady and Bill Belichick were about to be the first quarterback-coach duo to participate in five Super Bowls together. Tom had, once again, surpassed his idol Joe Montana. And in this particular Super Bowl, Tom would fittingly get a shot at the team who had given him his first Super Bowl loss, the New York Giants, and the quarterback who had compared himself to Tom in the preseason, Eli Manning.

The lead up to Super Bowl XLVI in Indianapolis underscored one thing for sure: Tom Brady had been in a lot of Super Bowls. It seemed like the media had run out of stuff to ask him. He talked about what was on TV in his house (*Toy Story 3*), his dance skills (poor), the quality of Buffalo hotels ("not the best"), and life growing up as a younger brother (his nails got painted once). One guy at media day even showed up in wizard's robes and offered to help Tom harness the energy of the dragon.

"Keep your dragon to yourself," Tom joked.

The Giants, on the other hand, weighed in on a more pressing subject: how to beat number twelve. "Tom Brady is a great quarterback," said Giants defensive end Jason Pierre-Paul. "But at the end of the day he is just a quarterback. It's not like he is God, he can't be touched."

Indeed, the Giants avoided Tom's divine wrath for almost the entire first half. On the first drive, the Patriots took over on their own six, and an intentional grounding penalty from Tom caused the referees to call a safety (when an offensive team is down in its own end zone)—the Giants got two points and the ball back. Manning took advantage and threw for a score, giving New York the rare 9–0 lead in football.

Gostkowski kicked a field goal to cut the lead to 9–3. Then, with four minutes left in the half, Tom led a masterful fourteen-play drive down nearly the entire length of the field. Having started from his own four-yard line, Tom soon found himself on the Giants' four-yard line. On third and four with fifteen seconds left in the half, Tom dropped back. With plenty of time, he rolled right and scanned his targets, looking from receiver to receiver. Finally, he found running back Danny Woodhead open just behind the goal line. Touchdown! Tom pumped his fist and screamed in excitement.

After Madonna's halftime show, Tom went right back to work, opening up the third quarter with another touchdown throw in the red zone: 17–9. Tom pointed with his right hand to the letters "MHK" stitched on his jersey and with his left hand toward the sky. The initials stood for Myra Hiatt Kraft, the wife of Pats owner Robert Kraft, who had died from cancer before the season.

In the third quarter, the Giants' pass rush finally got to Tom. Unlike in Super Bowl XLII, in which New York's defensive ends sacked Tom five times, he had enjoyed a very clean pocket all day to that point. The Giants kicked two field goals to cut the lead to 17–15. Then with four minutes left in the game, Tom dropped back on second and eleven only to find Wes Welker wide open on the Giants' twenty-five. Welker leapt for the ball, put both hands on it—and dropped it.

The Patriots had to punt. And on the first play of

the resulting drive, Eli Manning completed an unbelievable thirty-eight-yard pass down the sideline. With 1:09 left on the clock, down by just two, and on the Pats' seven-yard line, the Giants intended to run the clock down and then kick a game-winning field goal. New York running back Ahmad Bradshaw ran up the middle and tried to stop short of the goal line before tumbling backward for the touchdown. The Giants now led 21–17, but they had left Tom Brady an entire minute on the clock.

On his first down, Tom threw a line drive, but it was dropped around midfield. On second down, he hit another target on the hands. Again the ball hit the turf. And on third down, the Giants' pass rush got to Tom, sacking him before he could even look downfield. The Patriots took their final time-out. On fourth and sixteen, the pocket collapsed again. Tom eluded the oncoming Giants, moved to his left, and found an open man nineteen yards downfield. After another short completion, Tom spiked the ball on his own forty-four to stop the clock with nineteen seconds left.

His first pass attempt, on second down, was caught, but by a receiver out of bounds. With five seconds left, he threw a Hail Mary. It made it all the way to the end zone. It was tipped up in the air. Gronkowski dove for it . . . and missed. The ball rolled out of bounds. The Giants had beaten the Patriots in the Super Bowl again. Three crucial dropped passes had doomed the Pats.

After the game, Welker blamed himself, citing the ball that went through his hands with four minutes left. Tom's wife, Gisele, was overheard blaming the receivers, too, saying her husband couldn't "throw the ball and catch the ball at the same time."

For his part, Tom blamed nobody. After the game, he said they had lost together, as a team. He downplayed Welker's role in the crucial drop and said he would keep throwing his favorite target the ball for as long as he had the opportunity. Despite the pain of the loss, Tom showed leadership by letting his teammates know how he felt about them.

"We fought to the end, and I'm proud of that."

CHAPTER FIFTEEN

★ 2012–2013 ★

BECOMING AGELESS

Until recently, Tom Brady had never eaten a strawberry.

Despite everything he has accomplished, that may be the most remarkable fact about Tom: he claims to have never once tried the triangular red fruit (at least until a late-night TV host challenged him to try one in 2018). In fact, Tom Brady never eats fruit at all, if you exclude the bananas and blueberries he throws in his shakes. He also doesn't consume tomatoes, mushrooms, eggplants, any dairy, caffeine, salt, white sugar, or flour. (Don't worry, you can eat tomatoes and still grow up to be an NFL quarterback!)

Tom is not a picky eater. He has a personal and extremely specific nutritional reason for excluding each foodstuff. (He might cite, for instance, the belief that tomatoes are not anti-inflammatory.) His diet is just one aspect of the meticulous lifestyle he leads in order to continue playing football into and past his late thirties.

He was not always this focused on his health. Then again, Tom wasn't always this good at football. After every season starting in 2011, pundits would wonder aloud how much Tom Brady had left in the tank. And despite his age, Tom became more athletic, more prepared. And the Patriots became more consistent, winning exactly twelve games in each of the next four seasons from 2012 to 2015.

Tom's attitudes toward nutrition and fitness changed forever in 2006. He was dealing with a nagging groin injury. The team told him to undergo surgery. A teammate, linebacker Willie McGinest, advised him to see Alex Guerrero. Though he is not a doctor, Guerrero worked on Tom using his "body work" technique, which looks like a very intense massage. After Guerrero's technique helped him avoid surgery on his groin, Tom employed Guerrero again during his recovery from MCL and ACL surgery in 2008.

Alex and Tom became best friends, and together, worked tirelessly to extend the quarterback's career. The godfather of Tom's son Ben, Guerrero works on Brady's muscles and tendons every day and helps him plan his meals and workouts. Together, the two would launch TB12, a business focused on teaching people the secrets of Tom's lifestyle, with a fitness center located near the Patriots' home stadium.

Tom's nonstop commitment to his health may seem intense. He works out tirelessly on vacations. He plans off-season retreats with his wide receivers that are elaborate excuses to fine-tune the offense. His idea of a treat is sugarless, dairy-free avocado "ice cream." Tom had worked harder than the rest of the NFL to rise from college nonprospect to perennial All-Pro. Now, he was trying to achieve unprecedented career longevity. His idol, Joe Montana, had won four Super Bowls. Why would Tom retire satisfied with three?

That's why, entering the 2012 season, Tom Brady was as good as ever at age thirty-five, a birthday at which most quarterbacks begin to succumb to injuries, decline, or both. Another sign of aging: Tom welcomed his third child into the world that season, a daughter named Vivian Lake Brady. As incredible as it may have seemed at the time, Tom would still be the best quarterback in the league by the time Vivian reached kindergarten.

The average NFL career is only a little over three years long. Tom may not have changed in his thirteenth season, but the league had. There were new rivals. One of them was the Seattle Seahawks, and cornerback Richard Sherman in particular. Sherman had not even been in high school when Tom won his first Super Bowl. Sherman loved to talk... and he backed it up. He had quickly emerged as one of the league's best players.

In week three, the Patriots played the Seahawks in Seattle. With both teams at 3–2, the Pats seemed destined to win until late in the fourth quarter. The Seahawks scored twice and won 24–23. Tom had been unable to answer late. He threw two interceptions in the game, including one to Sherman.

"I kept saying I'm going to get that next time," Sherman said after the game. "Every TV time-out, I went up and said it right to [Tom]: 'Please keep trying me. I'm going to take it from you.' That was when they were winning. He just gave me that look and said, 'Oh, I'll see you after game.' Well, I made sure I saw him after the game."

In fact, Sherman tweeted a photo of him going up to Tom after the game and added the caption "U MAD BRO?" He deleted the tweet, but the message had been sent. As the Seahawks were nonconference opponents, the Patriots would not get their shot at getting the Seahawks back for another three years.

That next meeting, however, would be no ordinary game for Tom.

In the meantime, the Patriots and Tom did what they always seemed to do. They turned a .500 start to the season into another first-place finish. After their usual first-round bye in the playoffs, Tom and company dismantled the Houston Texans in their first playoff game. Tom threw for 344 yards and three touchdowns.

In the AFC Championship game against the Ravens, an early lead would fall apart. After falling behind 28–13, Tom would turn the ball over on downs and throw two interceptions. Baltimore went on to win the Super Bowl that season, linebacker Ray Lewis's last on the team. Lewis, a future Hall of Famer, had been a longtime rival of Tom's on the field—the two had jawed at each other, face masks interlocked, in some tense games. But Lewis, like so many of Brady's contemporaries, was done with football. Tom kept going

It wasn't just longtime opponents of Tom who began to disappear during this era. Before the 2013 season, just as had happened before 2006, Tom lost his two most productive receivers from the year before, Wes Welker and Brandon Lloyd. Welker signed with the Broncos during the off-season; Lloyd took a year off from football before joining the San Francisco 49ers.

This time, however, the Patriots did not need to go find another Randy Moss. Julian Edelman had taken over for Welker on punt returns years earlier, when Welker had been injured. Like Tom, Edelman had been overlooked coming out of college, picked by the Patriots in the seventh round of the 2009 draft. A converted wide receiver, Edelman had played quarterback at Kent State. Like Tom had in 2001, Edelman made the most of his opportunity in 2013, going from 235 receiving yards the season before to 1,056. Tom dubbed his new favorite target "Minitron," a play on the nickname of Lions superstar Calvin "Megatron" Johnson, who is five inches taller than Edelman.

There was, of course, one notable former Tom Brady foe who had also defied Father Time. Peyton Manning's Colts career ended after he missed the entire 2011 season following spinal fusion surgery. His doctors informed him that, at his age, the surgery could very well end his NFL career. In 2012, however, Manning signed with the Denver Broncos. And by 2013, at age thirty-seven, he broke Tom's single-season touchdown record, throwing fifty-five. He also broke Drew Brees's single-season passing yards record—set during the "Year of the Quarterback"—by one yard. Manning also had a secret weapon that year: Wes Welker.

Tom, meanwhile, statistically had one of his worst seasons in years, throwing for just twenty-five touchdowns and eleven interceptions. Multiple injuries, including a season-ending ACL/MCL tear, limited Rob Gronkowski, Tom's best red-zone target, to just seven games. It was only fitting, then, with Tom and Peyton putting up numbers like their younger selves, that they would meet in the AFC Championship game.

Unfortunately, not everything went like old times. Far removed from the great Patriot defenses that tormented Manning in snowy Foxborough, the Broncos QB put on a show in sunny Denver. Tom got a pair of fourth-quarter touchdowns, but it was too little too late. Denver won 26–16, then got blown out in Super Bowl XLVIII, 43–8. There was a new power in the NFL: Richard Sherman's Seahawks.

CHAPTER SIXTEEN

★ 2014 ★

MOTIVATED

With the sixty-second pick in the 2014 draft, the Patriots selected Jimmy Garoppolo, a quarterback out of Eastern Illinois. The Patriots hadn't taken a quarterback that early since they picked Drew Bledsoe first overall in 1993.

After the draft, Belichick explained the pick by saying, "We know what Tom's age and contract situation is."

Tom's contract situation was complicated and ever-changing, with Tom making concessions on guaranteed money to give the franchise more flexibility with the salary cap. But his age? Tom was not concerned with that. And he wasn't keen to let Garoppolo do to him what he had done to Bledsoe.

The Pats' rookie QB would get his first work in Game 4 of the 2014 season. The Patriots lost a blowout to the Kansas City Chiefs, 41–13. Garoppolo made six of seven pass attempts in mop-up duty.

The Patriots fell to 2–2, and, once again, eager

naysayers called it the end of the Pats' dynasty. After the game, a reporter even asked Bill Belichick, "Will the quarterback position be evaluated this week?" In other words, was he going to bench Brady? Belichick gave the inquiring party a cold stare before letting out a chuckle.

"There's nothing better that can happen to get [Tom]'s competitive juices going," Robert Kraft would later tell NFL Films. "So thank you to all the people and media people who did that."

Tom's competitive juices propelled the Patriots to yet another 12–4, AFC East–leading finish. Despite all their success, however, it had been an entire decade since their last championship win. Tom and his team had only one goal.

Their first opponent in the playoffs was a familiar antagonist, the Baltimore Ravens. At home in Gillette Stadium, it almost looked like a repeat of 2009. The Ravens went up 28–14 in the third quarter.

Desperate, the Patriots called a trick play named "Baltimore." The Patriots lined up with just four linemen, with tight end Michael Hoomanawanui posing as a tackle. Hoomanawanui went uncovered and the play led to a solid sixteen-yard gain. That convinced Belichick and Tom to try a different version of the play, called "Raven." That one worked, too, again for a modest gain. That drive led to a five-yard touchdown pass from Tom to Rob. They cut the lead in half, to 28–21.

When the Pats got the ball back after a quick three-and-out from Baltimore, the Patriots got even trickier. Tom threw backward to Julian Edelman, who then used his skills as a former college quarterback to throw downfield. The ball found receiver Danny Amendola, wide open past the twenty! He ran the rest of the way to the end zone. Tie game.

The Patriots had all the momentum. After the Ravens could only muster a field goal in response, Tom drove his team seventy-four yards for a touchdown. New England was moving on.

The AFC Championship game against the Colts would lead to two career-defining moments for Tom. It was a lopsided 45–7 Patriots win, in which Tom threw two touchdowns. It was also the game that started "Deflategate."

After the game, reports surfaced that the Patriots had cheated by illegally deflating footballs below allowable levels. In theory, less inflated footballs are easier to grip and throw, meaning Tom would stand to benefit from having his game balls less pumped up than his opponent's.

It didn't help that the Patriots had previously dealt with accusations of bending the rules during the Belichick era. While Tom had nothing to do with it, the Pats were caught illegally taping the signals of Jets coaches in 2007. Belichick had been fined $500,000 and the team had forfeited a first-round pick. The Patriots' tremendous success during the Belichick-Brady era, combined with that history of "Spygate," made opposing fans eager to label them as cheaters.

"Deflategate" became a huge story leading up to Super Bowl XLIX. Tom could not give it any mind. He had to focus on the big game, against the Seahawks, a team he had not faced since the "U MAD BRO?" tweet. In addition to it being ten years since their last title, the Patriots would get a chance to play another Super Bowl in Arizona's University of Phoenix Stadium, where the Giants had ruined their perfect season in January 2008.

In the game, Tom struck first. Early in the second quarter, he found receiver Brandon LaFell for an eleven-yard scoring strike. When the Seahawks came back with a rushing touchdown from superstar running back Marshawn Lynch, Tom had an answer. After advancing to the Seahawks' twenty-two-yard line, Tom saw a linebacker covering Gronk. The big tight end outraced his defender and then caught the ball over the Seahawk player's head.

The Seahawks re-tied the game before halftime, then added a touchdown and a field goal at the beginning of the third quarter to grab a 24–14 advantage. As Tom walked up and down the sideline ready to go back in, he called out to his offense, "Hey, we've been in worse situations than this, huh?" He had reason to act cool. He had been here before.

With less than nine minutes to go, Tom got his team all the way down to the Seattle four. On first and goal, Edelman made a great move to cause his defender to fall down and get wide open in the end zone. Tom saw him—he just missed the pass. Still, he hit Amendola for the score on the very next play. 24–21.

After the Seahawks punted on the following drive, Tom again drove his offense to the red zone, this time getting to Seattle's three-yard line. At Tom's behest, the Patriots ran the same play that had gotten Edelman open in the same situation earlier.

Again, he shook his man. This time, Tom didn't miss. The pass hit him right on the hands. Touchdown! The Patriots went up 28–24.

The Seahawks had two minutes to drive downfield and win the Super Bowl. Seattle made it into New England territory quickly, but down by four, they needed six points, not a kick. Seahawks QB Russell Wilson threw deep to wide receiver Jermaine Kearse. Patriots cornerback Malcolm Butler got a hand on the ball and broke up the play. As Kearse and Butler fell to the turf, however, the Seahawks receiver hit the ball in the air twice and, lying on his back, reeled it in.

It had happened again. In Arizona, in the Super Bowl, the Patriots had a lead, only to see their opponents connect on one of the most miraculous catches of all time. Tom could only shake his head with a look of disbelief from the sideline.

The Seahawks had the ball on the Pats' one-yard line with three chances to punch it in. They also had Lynch, the league's most punishing running back, in their backfield. Tom stood on the sideline, hands on his hips, and watched. On second down, Wilson dropped back and threw to a wide-open receiver streaking toward the goal line. Then, Malcolm

Butler came out of nowhere. He jumped the route. Interception!

Tom jumped up and down screaming like a little kid. He grabbed offensive coordinator Josh McDaniels. "We did it, Josh!" On the field, as the confetti came down, Tom hugged his teammates. "We did it, bro. I love ya. I love ya," he told Edelman.

After ten years of greatness, the Patriots finally had won number four. Tom had matched Montana. Next up: passing him.

CHAPTER SEVENTEEN

★ 2015–2016 ★

THE FINAL SHOWDOWN

Tom Brady was free! On September 3, 2015, the city of Boston celebrated the return of their quarterback.

In May, the NFL had announced a four-game suspension for Tom, related to the "Deflategate" scandal. An independent investigation into the circumstances surrounding the underinflated footballs the Patriots used against the Colts in the AFC Championship game had found it "more probable than not" that Tom had known that the balls were being deflated. Commissioner Roger Goodell then suspended Tom, citing Tom's refusal to produce emails or texts related to the incident to investigators.

Ironically, Tom had pushed for a rule change that made the incident possible, way back in 2006. Tom and Peyton Manning had teamed up to petition the league office to allow quarterbacks on the away team more control over the condition of the balls they use. The home team, to that point, had been charged with rubbing the slick shine off the balls.

Tom did not let any air out of any footballs. But he destroyed the cellphone that possibly contained text messages to the two men who did. Tom claimed he routinely destroyed his cell phone for security reasons. Still, the commissioner upheld Tom's suspension on appeal. The Patriots' star released a statement in which he denied the accusations.

"I am very disappointed by the NFL's decision to uphold the four-game suspension against me," Tom wrote. "I did nothing wrong, and no one in the Patriots organization did either."

The NFL Players Association appealed the suspension in court. There, a judge vacated it, allowing Tom to play the entire 2015 season. The legal battle was not over, but for the time being, Tom Brady could play football.

The rest of the NFL was probably angry at that judge. Tom won the first ten games of the season. The Patriots finished first in their division for the seventh year in a row. And for the fourth and final time, Tom Brady and Peyton Manning would face off in the AFC Championship game for the right to advance to the Super Bowl.

This matchup, however, figured to be different. At age thirty-eight, Brady had posted a passer rating over 100 (102.2) for the fourth time in his career. He had led the league in touchdowns with thirty-six.

Manning, by contrast, had a poor 67.9 passer rating after his 101.5 the year before. He had thrown seventeen interceptions to just nine touchdowns in nine starts during the regular season and had a 59.8 percent completion percentage, his lowest since his rookie season in 1998. Manning had even had to win his job back from backup Brock Osweiler late in the season.

Manning showed in this game that he had at least something left in the tank. Midway through the first quarter, he hit tight end Owen Daniels for a touchdown pass down the middle. He then found Daniels again with a soft lob to the right side of the end zone in the second quarter to put the Broncos up 14–6.

Brady, meanwhile, felt the pressure from Denver's pass rush. They would sack Tom four times, and hit him more often than that. Off his game, Tom threw two interceptions in the first half.

In the second half, both defenses played well. With two minutes left in the game, Tom would find himself needing eight points to tie, down 20–12. He did the hard part, getting his team down the field. Then, on fourth and goal from the four-yard line,

Tom took the snap. With a Broncos lineman bearing down on him, he made a desperate heave to the end zone, where Rob Gronkowski appeared from behind a defender to make the catch with twelve seconds left in the game. Touchdown! But the Pats would have to go for the two-point conversion.

Tom dropped back. The Broncos pass rushers closed fast, and Tom rolled right. He threw for Edelman, but the ball was batted in the air, then intercepted.

Manning had gotten the final win of their storied matchup, and his Broncos would go on to win the Super Bowl behind that same strong pass rush. After the AFC Championship game, Manning and Tom hugged and shook hands in the middle of the field, surrounded by photographers. Manning would retire after the season. He finished his career 6–11 against Tom.

CHAPTER EIGHTEEN

★ 2016 ★

THE COMEBACK

In week three of the 2016 season, the Patriots quarterback led his team to their third consecutive win. Granted, he only threw for 103 yards that game, on just nineteen attempts. He could be forgiven, though. He was, after all, just a rookie, a third-round pick out of North Carolina State named Jacoby Brissett.

Tom's "Deflategate" suspension had been reinstated. He would sit out four games after all. And in his stead, Jimmy Garoppolo had played brilliantly, until getting hurt in week two. That meant Brissett had to take over for two weeks until the face of the Patriots' franchise returned.

In the meanwhile, Tom could neither practice with nor have any contact with his teammates. So he took the time to mend a relationship with an old team of his: the Michigan Wolverines.

Tom never forgot the way the coaches and fans in Michigan seemed to have always been eager to replace him with another QB. Now, however, Tom

Brady was the greatest quarterback to ever play the game of football. The university of course wanted to embrace him as one of their greatest sports alumni.

So at the invitation of the school, Tom and nine-year-old Jack went to Ann Arbor to watch the Wolverines take on the Colorado Buffaloes. Before the game, he tried to pump up the team.

"It was a chilling speech," one pumped-up Michigan player told ESPN. "It made the hair on the back of your neck stand up."

Before kickoff, Michigan showed highlights from his career. Tom stood and waved as the Big House showed its gratitude.

No crowd was happier to welcome him back than the one in Gillette Stadium. Tom returned in week four on the road and threw for 406 yards in a win against Cleveland. Then he played his first game back in Foxborough the next week and threw three touchdowns in a win against Cincinnati. Tom had not fallen behind during the suspension. He was better than ever.

Tom went 11–1 in his twelve starts. He threw twenty-eight touchdown passes and just two interceptions. His 112.2 passer rating was the second best of his career, but it was second in the league that year to Atlanta's Matt Ryan. Behind Ryan, the Falcons seemed like a team of destiny. He led them to two consecutive blowout wins (against the Seahawks and the Packers) in the playoffs. The team they would face in the Super Bowl, however, had a hot offense of its own.

The Patriots scored seventy total points in the first two rounds of the 2016 postseason. In the AFC Championship game against the Steelers, Tom threw for 384 yards and three touchdowns. He was now 13–1 since his suspension.

At Super Bowl media day, Tom dodged the usual questions from wizards about dragons. Instead a seven-year-old kid reporter asked Tom who his hero was. Tom's eyes welled with tears.

"I think my dad is my hero because he's someone I look up to every day," he said.

Tom was thinking about his parents even more than usual before this particular championship. His mom, Galynn, had begun treatment that season for cancer. Tom had stayed positive, though, telling his mom, "You'll be ready for the Super Bowl." She was.

Super Bowl LI started as yet another playoff rout...for the Falcons. Atlanta went up 14–0 after consecutive scoring drives in the second quarter. Tom responded by driving into Falcon territory. On third and six, from the Atlanta twenty-three, Tom dropped back and threw underneath to Danny Amendola. The pass was intercepted. Falcons cornerback Robert Alford ran in front of Amendola and took the ball eighty-two yards to the end zone.

The Patriots kicked a field goal right before the half, and then Matt Ryan threw another touchdown pass to start the third quarter. The Falcons had twenty-three minutes to defend a twenty-five-point lead, up 28–3. By one calculation, the Falcons had a 99.9 percent win probability. ESPN would even devote an entire segment the next season to New England fans who had left the game in Houston early.

There was one person who wasn't ready to leave. On the sideline, Tom began to address his teammates. They recognized a familiar tone in his voice, the one he used when they were sorely in need of a leader. With his helmet back on and ready to go, he gave his troops a simple message: "No fear, cut it loose."

On third and three on their own forty-six, New England tried the "double pass," in which Edelman got to make a throw. It fell incomplete. So on fourth down in the third quarter of the Super Bowl, Tom had to go for it. He found Amendola on the sideline. First down. Less than a minute later, facing third and eight, Tom ran out of the pocket to escape an oncoming Falcons pass rusher. Suddenly, the quarterback with the historically bad forty-yard-dash time at age twenty-two was tucking the ball in and running at thirty-nine. He slid after fifteen yards.

Following some tough running from Pats back LaGarrette Blount, the offense was on Atlanta's five. Tom threw short to running back James White, who dove for the goal line. Touchdown! They missed the extra point, making it 28–9 with seventeen minutes to go.

After the Falcons had to punt, Tom made five passes to get down to the Falcons' seven-yard line. There, however, he would be sacked twice. Gostkowski made a thirty-three-yard field goal. The score was 28–12 with less than ten minutes to go.

On their ensuing drive, the Falcons had third and one on their own thirty-six. Instead of running the ball to pick up that last yard and keep the clock ticking, they strangely dropped back to pass. New England's defense made them pay. Linebacker Dont'a Hightower came around the right edge and knocked the ball loose with a huge hit on Ryan. The Patriots fell on the fumble! Tom would get the ball back in Atlanta territory.

He took advantage. He made three quick consecutive passes. Then, on second and two from the six, Danny Amendola ran an out route along the goal line. Tom hit him perfectly. Touchdown. The offense hustled back to the line as Tom held up his index and middle fingers, signally for the two-point conversion. They snapped the ball directly to running back James White as Tom pretended to miss the ball. He ran straight up the middle. In! It was now just 28–20 with less than six minutes to go.

Suddenly, the Falcons had a big problem. They bled a couple minutes off the clock, but giving Tom Brady 3:30 to score one touchdown was not going to cut it. On first and ten, from his own thirty-six, Tom threw deep across the field to Julian Edelman. An Atlanta defender tipped the ball in the air. Edelman dove across three Falcons to snatch it, seeming to bobble it as it hit the ground. The officials signaled catch! Sure enough, instant replay showed Edelman catch it, drop it, and then catch it again just before it hit the ground. Finally, the Patriots were *making* the miraculous catches late in the Super Bowl, not giving them up.

Tom threw twenty yards to Amendola on first down, and then thirteen yards to White. On first and goal from the eight, he found White again, but the running back was stopped just short of the end zone. So next play, Tom handed him the ball, and White punched it in. Tom raised both arms. Touchdown. There was never any doubt.

Still, the Patriots were down two points. Danny Amendola, out wide to the left, went in motion pre-snap, running toward Tom. His quarterback got him the ball on a screen pass. Amendola ran toward the end zone, colliding with Falcons defenders. The ball barely broke the plane. It was good! Suddenly, the game was tied 28–28.

The Super Bowl went to overtime for the first time ever. The Patriots called "heads" and won the first overtime coin toss in Super Bowl history. New England felt confident. Why shouldn't they? Julian Edelman turned to Tom on the sideline and said, "Let's go score and win this thing, baby...for your mom. For your mom, bro." The quarterback nodded, a resolved look on his face.

Overtime rules stated that a field goal would give the Falcons a chance to answer. A touchdown ended the game. Tom came out firing. He made a great throw to Amendola's back shoulder to pick up a quick fourteen yards. He then found receiver Chris

Hogan to cross midfield. Next Tom went to Minitron, up the middle for fifteen. With the ball on the Atlanta fifteen, Tom went for the end zone, tossing a lob into the arms of tight end Martellus Bennett. The ball hit the turf.

But there was a flag on the play! Pass interference on the defense moved the ball up to the two-yard line. On second and goal, Tom pitched the ball right to White. He had blockers. A Falcons defender grabbed onto his waist near the line of scrimmage. He kept going. With three players dragging him down, he reached for the goal line. Touchdown!

The Patriots players went crazy, except Tom. The savvy and unflappable veteran urged his teammates to wait for the instant replay to confirm the touchdown. But the score would stand. The Comeback Kid had just led the greatest comeback in the history of the game. No team had ever overcome more than a ten-point deficit in the Super Bowl. Tom had made up twenty-five, and in less than half a game.

"He's laser-focused, and the entire time, there wasn't a time where we looked at Tom like he knew this thing was over," Chris Hogan said afterward. "There wasn't a doubt in my mind. We have one of the best quarterbacks that ever played the game."

Maybe he was *the* best. Tom Brady's childhood idol Joe Montana had won four Super Bowls and three game MVP awards. Tom now had five rings and four Super Bowl MVP trophies.

He stood alone in history. On the field, he stood with his family: his kids, wife, dad, and ebullient mom, for whom he had won the game.

CHAPTER NINETEEN

★ 2017 and Beyond ★

TB12 FOREVER

Tom Brady did not win Super Bowl LII against the Eagles the next season. Philadelphia's offense knocked around New England's defense. Another quarterback—Nick Foles—got to play Tom's role, leading key fourth-quarter drives. The Patriots lost, 41–33.

But consider some amazing facts about Tom's 2017 season. He was forty years old. He was the oldest player (excluding kickers) to ever play in the game. And still he set the record for passing yards in a single Super Bowl (505), breaking a record previously set by... Tom Brady, at thirty-nine years old, the year before.

During the regular season, the Pats tied for the best record in football (13–3). Tom led the league in passing yards (4,577) and won his third MVP award. Tom had outlasted his contemporaries. And now in his forties with no intention of stopping, he had started schooling a whole new generation of opposing quarterbacks and defenses.

Still, there were signs of strain in Foxborough. As Tom released a book detailing his health and lifestyle—*The TB12 Method*—Belichick banned his friend and business partner Alex Guerrero from the team's sideline and plane. (The Patriots have their own full-time training staff.) Belichick also traded Jimmy Garoppolo, his chosen successor to Brady. No one would be turning Tom into Drew Bledsoe. Tom wouldn't allow it. He refused to age like a normal human being.

Despite all the rumors, the Patriots remain a powerhouse. Tom has a contract that runs through 2019, and he shows no signs of slowing down. An ESPN report about the team's drama, released before the Super Bowl, carried a familiar question in its headline: "For Kraft, Brady and Belichick, is this the beginning of the end?"

Don't count on it.

Tom Brady had worked tirelessly to earn a spot in the NFL that thirty-one other teams didn't want to give him. He now works equally hard to get an ending that's on his terms, too. Just don't expect it to come anytime soon.

Serra High School (San Mateo, CA)

High school quarterback Tom Brady throws the ball in 1995.

In his University of Michigan maize and blue, Tom makes a pass at a 1999 game against the University of Wisconsin—Madison.

John Biever/*Sports Illustrated*/Getty Images

Jim Davis/*The Boston Globe* via Getty Images

The final game at Foxboro Stadium was the famously snowy 2001 AFC divisional-round playoff game between the Patriots and the Raiders—which the Pats won in an overtime thriller. Here, Tom (#12) loses the ball after being hit by the Raiders' Charles Woodson.

Tom in action against the St. Louis Rams, during Super Bowl XXXVI in 2002.

John Iacono /*Sports Illustrated*/Getty Images

Jamie Squire/Getty Images

Celebrating a big win! Joined on the field by his wife, Gisele Bündchen, and sons, Jack and Benjamin, during Super Bowl XLIX, Tom celebrates defeating the Seattle Seahawks, 28–24, in 2015.

Al Tielemans /*Sports Illustrated*/Getty Images

The MVP in action during Super Bowl LI in 2017, passing the ball against the Atlanta Falcons

Tom raises the Vince Lombardi Trophy in triumph after defeating the Atlanta Falcons in a 34–28 overtime win during Super Bowl LI.

AP Photo/Darron Cummings

★ TOM BRADY'S ★ SELECT YEAR-TO-YEAR HIGHLIGHTS

1998
Citrus Bowl champion
Big Ten team title
1999
Second Team All-Big Ten
University of Michigan Team MVP
Orange Bowl champion
2000
Sixth round NFL draft pick
2001
Super Bowl XXXVI champion
Super Bowl XXXVI MVP
Pro Bowler
2002
Led the league in touchdown passes (28)
Made Team Captain

2003
Super Bowl XXXVIII champion
Super Bowl XXXVIII MVP
2004
Super Bowl XXXIX champion
Sporting News Sportsman of the Year
Pro Bowler
2005
Sports Illustrated Sportsman of the Year
Pro Bowler
Led the league in passing yards (4,110)
2007
NFL MVP
Offensive Player of the Year
First Team All-Pro
Associated Press Male Athlete of the Year
Sporting News Sportsman of the Year
NFL Alumni Quarterback of the Year

AFC Offensive Player of the Year
AFC Champion
Pro Bowler
Led the league in passing yards (4,806)
Led the league in passer rating (117.2)
Single-season passing touchdown record (50)
2009
Associated Press Comeback Player of the Year
Pro Bowler
2010
NFL MVP
Offensive Player of the Year
First Team All-Pro
Sporting News All-Pro
Pro Bowler
Led the league in passer rating (111.0)
2011
AFC Champion
Pro Bowler

2012
Pro Bowler
2013
Pro Bowler
2014
Super Bowl XLIX Champion
Super Bowl XLIX MVP
Pro Football Writers Association All-AFC Team
Pro Bowler
2015
Pro Bowler
2016
Super Bowl LI Champion
Super Bowl LI MVP
Second Team All-Pro
Sporting News Offensive Player of the Year
Pro Football Writers Association All-AFC Team
Pro Bowler

2017
NFL MVP
AFC Champion
Led the league in passing yards (4,577)
Threw for 505 yards in Super Bowl LII, an NFL record
Pro Bowler

Turn the page to start another exciting sports biography

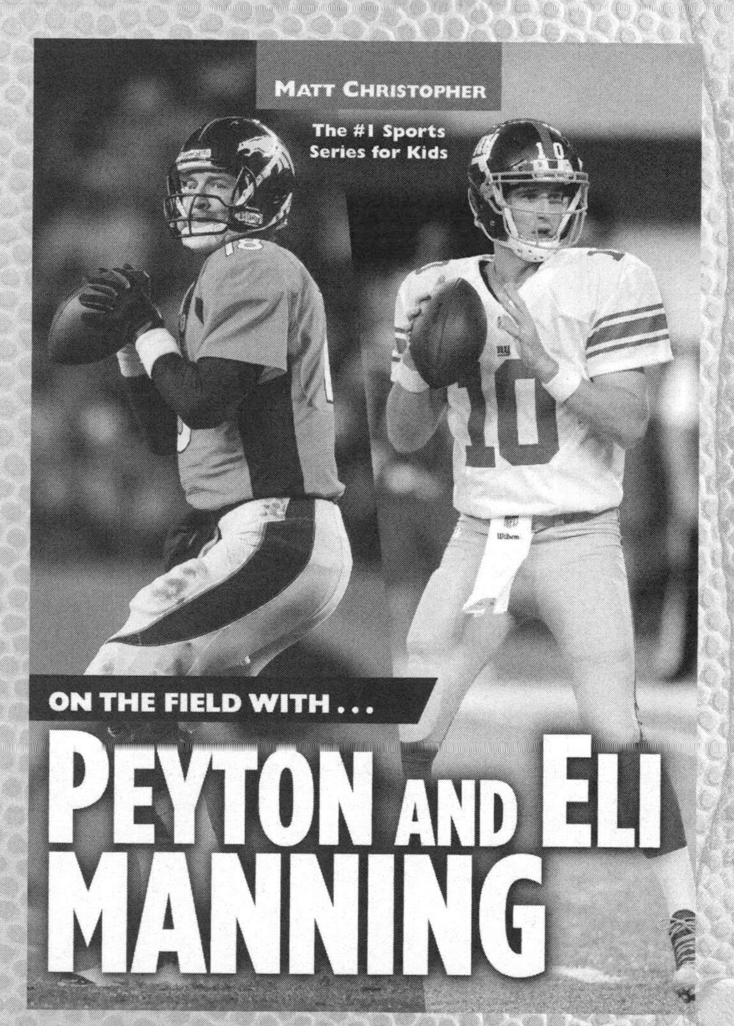

✯ PROLOGUE ✯

What Is a Dynasty?

Dictionaries describe a dynasty as an influential family that obtains and keeps power for more than one generation. Sometimes that power is political, such as that handed down from kings and queens to their children, or when the son or daughter of a government leader follows in his or her parent's footsteps. Sometimes the dynasty begins with a successful entrepreneur who passes the business on to his or her children. A dynasty can also be a family of popular actors and actresses, or musicians, or artists.

When people use the term dynasty in the sports world, usually they mean a team has had several championship years in a row. For example, the Chicago Bulls ruled the National Basketball Association from 1991 to 1998, posting six titles. The New York Yankees have had two dynastic eras, one from 1936 to 1943 and one from 1947 to 1962, racking up a grand total of 16 World Series victories. The Green

Bay Packers were untouchable from 1961 to 1967, as were the Pittsburgh Steelers from 1974 to 1979.

The sporting world has family dynasties, too, although they are not as common. After all, just because a father or a mother is a great athlete doesn't mean their children — or nieces, nephews, brothers, sisters, or other relatives — will be.

Then again, growing up with a sports star gives others in the family certain advantages. Children get an up close and personal look at how a sport is played, for one thing. They learn the finer points of the sport from a very early age and see what an athlete must do to reach the top of his or her game. Armed with this knowledge, the next generation is poised to step in when the previous one is ready to retire.

Such was the case with Major League Baseball's Ken Griffey Sr. and Ken Griffey Jr. This father-and-son duo not only excelled in the same sport, they played on the same team — and in 1990, in several of the same games, including one in which they hit back-to-back homers! (Ken Jr.'s younger brother, Craig, was also a ballplayer, although his career began and ended in the minors.)

NASCAR also has a family dynasty, the Earnhardts. The late Dale Earnhardt Sr. was one of the most popular and skillful drivers of the 1980s and

90s. His sons, Dale Jr. and Kerry, followed him into racing and have each had successful careers; his older daughter, Kelley, is Dale Jr.'s manager and business agent.

The list goes on: slugger Barry Bonds of Major League Baseball is the son of former MLB great Bobby Bonds. Muhammad Ali's daughter, Laila, is now a professional boxer, like her father. Jimmy Walker, father of NBA superstar Jalen Rose, played for three NBA teams in the 1960s and 1970s. Former National Football League tight end Don Hasselbeck is the father of two current NFL quarterbacks: Tim, of the Arizona Cardinals, and Matt, of the Seattle Seahawks.

Amazingly, the Hasselbeck trio is not the only father-son-son dynasty in the NFL currently. The other is that of the Mannings: Archie, Peyton, and Eli. This is the story of their dynasty's path to greatness.

✯ CHAPTER ONE ✯

1949–1967

Archie

Archie Manning, father of NFL quarterbacks Peyton and Eli, has lived in New Orleans, Louisiana, since 1971. But he doesn't consider himself as from that city.

"When anyone asks me where I'm from," he once told a reporter, "I say Drew."

"Drew" is Drew, Mississippi, a tiny, impoverished town in the northwest corner of the state, an area known as the Delta. Elisha Archibald Manning III was born there on May 19, 1949. His father, Buddy, worked for a farm machinery dealership. His mother, Sis, was a secretary for three town lawyers and "pretty much ran the town," according to Archie. Along with his older sister, Pam, they lived in a small wooden house that was actually three separate buildings that had been combined to form one dwelling.

Archie's childhood was fairly typical for the 1950s and 60s. He went to school, he did chores, he attended church and church school, and he got chocolate milk shakes at the local drugstore whenever he could. He also played sports — baseball, football, track, and basketball.

Baseball was Archie's favorite sport at first. He loved it so much, in fact, that one summer he constructed a baseball diamond between his backyard and his neighbor's so that he and his friends could play every day. "It had some lumps and bumps," Archie said of the field, "but all the measurements were correct and as far as I was concerned, it was beautiful."

Archie loved football, too. During one pickup game, the other kids made him their quarterback. After that, he never played another position if he could help it.

In the fifth grade, he joined the local peewee league. Archie remembers the terror of being a 70-pound pip-squeak facing opponents 50 pounds heavier and a few years older than him. But even the thought of being flattened by one of those boys never stopped him from playing.

"At that point I could run and throw the ball pretty well, and I hung in," he said.

Archie continued to play sports throughout his junior high and high school years. Football became his favorite, despite the fact that he seemed to get injured fairly often!

One injury came when he was a freshman. The coach told him that he'd be quarterbacking an upcoming game. Archie was thrilled. But his hopes were dashed when, the very next day, he broke his right arm during practice.

That break sidelined him for the rest of the season. Fortunately, he was back in action when his sophomore year rolled around. He made the roster as the backup quarterback. By the season's last game, he had moved into the starting position.

He started his junior year, too — for three games, anyway. Then, in the midst of the third, he was crushed beneath an opponent and broke his left arm. Another break, another season of sitting on the sidelines!

Despite the injuries, Archie had played enough — and been good enough — to get noticed by a few important people that year. He didn't know that, however, until the eve of his senior year in high school. It was then that his coach told him that some college recruiters would be watching him closely in his final season. If they liked what they saw, they might offer him a scholarship.

Archie had never really considered going to college,

let alone going on a football scholarship. Still, "the more I thought about it," he said, "the more excited I got."

That excitement transferred to the field. Drew High School's football team had never been one of the area's winning teams. But in 1966, with an injury-free Archie Manning at the helm, they won five out of their ten games, the most they'd won in years.

Soon after football ended, scholarship offers from a few colleges appeared. One was from the University of Mississippi. Archie had been a longtime fan of Ole Miss, and knew that the coach, Johnny Vaught, had a reputation for developing great quarterbacks. He saw no reason not to accept their offer.

It would turn out to be a match made in heaven.